Praise for *How to F...*
Company Ca...

"Glenn's messages resonate with my values and those that have made Staples so successful. This book is clear, direct, and right on target . . . a great source of useful career advice. Highly recommended."

> Ronald L. Sargent
> Chairman and CEO, Staples

"What a resource of practical advice based on facts, not anecdotes! The examples he provides perfectly illustrate what our grandparents have taught us. This book is a must read for all the different generations entering the workforce today."

> Samuel E. Beall, III
> Chairman and CEO, Ruby Tuesday

"Thank you for clearly focusing on the fact that hard work does pay off."

> Jack J. Pelton
> Chairman, President, and CEO,
> Cessna Aircraft Company

"Glenn presents the world's future entrepreneurs a clearly defined roadmap on building a better mousetrap!"

> Jim McCann
> CEO, 1-800-FLOWERS.COM®

"Anyone can succeed in America with an education and hard work. Glenn reminds us that the best employees are happy, honest, hard-working people."

> Steve Odland
> Chairman and CEO, Office Depot

"There are hundreds of books on how companies can create value for customers, but Glenn Shepard has given us a much-needed book on how employees can create value for their employers! He has written a clear, engaging, and compelling book on what it takes to create demand for yourself in the marketplace. Learn how to go from being 'overhead' and an expense to a company, to being an absolute necessity."

> Joe Calloway
> Author of *Indispensable—How to Become the*
> *Company That Your Customers Can't Live Without*
> Nashville, Tennessee
> www.JoeCalloway.com

"The most uplifting message of this book—and one that I stress with my employees—is that anyone can become indispensable to their company."

David Riklan
President, Self Improvement Online, Inc.
Marlboro, New Jersey
www.SelfGrowth.com

"This book should be in the top drawer of every employee's desk."

Matt Bacak, President
Frontier Power Marketing, LLC
Atlanta, Georgia
www.PowerfulPromoter.com

"The wisdom contained in this book can propel your career to new heights. Apply Glenn Shepard's techniques and be prepared to enjoy a phenomenally rewarding, exciting and positive work and career experience."

Peggy McColl
Author of *The 8 Proven Secrets to Smart Success*
Ottawa, Canada
www.Destinies.com

"Glenn has cleverly encapsulated the problem with our country's declining work ethic—and crafted the solution! Bravo Glenn!"

T. J. Marrs, President, The Creative Real Estate Source
Portland, Oregon
www.tjmarrs.com

"This book is like music to a manager's ears and should be integrated as part of the policy manual for every company. I wish I had written this one myself!"

Mike Stewart, President
SoundPages, Inc.
Atlanta, Georgia
www.TheInternetAudioGuy.com
www.TheInternetVideoGuy.com

How to Be the Employee Your Company Can't Live Without

18 Ways to Become Indispensable

GLENN SHEPARD

WILEY

John Wiley & Sons, Inc.

Published by John Wiley & Sons, Inc., Hoboken, New Jersey.
Published simultaneously in Canada.

For general information on our other products and services or for technical support, please contact our Customer Care Department within the United States at (800) 762-2974, outside the United States at (317) 572-3993 or fax (317) 572-4002.

This book is available for purchase in bulk quantities. Call (800) 538-4595 for details.

Wiley also publishes its books in a variety of electronic formats. Some content that appears in print may not be available in electronic books. For more information about Wiley products, visit our web site at www.wiley.com.

Library of Congress Cataloging-in-Publication Data:

Shepard, Glenn, 1963–
    How to be the employee your company can't live without: 18 ways to become indispensable / Glenn Shepard.
        p. cm.
    Includes bibliographical references and index.
    ISBN-13 978-0-471-75180-9 (pbk.)
    ISBN-10 0-471-75180-4 (pbk.)
    1. Career development. 2. Self-realization. 3. Vocational guidance. I. Title.
    HF5549.5C35S54   2006
    650.1—dc22
                                                          2005026319

Printed in the United States of America.
10 9 8 7 6 5 4 3 2 1

For all the hard-working people, white collar or blue, who bring pride, honor and dignity to a job well done.

Preface

This book equips you with the tools you need to succeed in getting a raise or promotion. It also offers something far more valuable, and it's something most books on how to get ahead in your career lack—how to stay there once you have arrived. This book provides the one thing you really need to know, which is how to be indispensable to your employer. It shows you how to get to where you want to be and how to stay there once you have arrived. Most of the principles contained within these pages are nothing more than common sense that society seems to have forgotten over the past few generations. They apply regardless of whether you're a custodian, surgeon, CEO, factory worker, or anything else.

My favorite book on leadership is *The 21 Irrefutable Laws of Leadership* by John C. Maxwell.[1] The principles in this book are also irrefutable regardless of your spiritual beliefs, political convictions, gender, or age.

You've already taken the first step toward becoming indispensable if you purchased this book for yourself. You are making an effort to increase your value to your company. This is more effort than average individuals will exert and it is why they will remain average. If your manager gave you this book, this may be the greatest career opportunity you'll ever have. He or she is handing you your future on a silver platter and all you have to do is take it. If a family member or friend gave this to you, he or she obviously wants you to succeed. I hope you'll show your appreciation for the concern for your success by taking advantage of the incredible career-changing power contained within these pages.

To do this, you'll need to understand who wrote this book. Who is Glenn Shepard and why should you take career advice from me? I'm not the pat-people-on-the-back and make-them-feel-good-about-themselves kind of author who typically writes books on this subject. I come to the field of career coaching from a unique perspective. You could say that I play both sides of the fence. I am the man who some consider to be the Grim Reaper of Employment. Through management seminars and in my last book, *How to Manage Problem Employees*,[2] I teach managers not to put off the decision to terminate troublemakers and poor performers who exhibit no desire to improve. Your boss may have even attended one of my seminars or read my previous books.

So why should you take career advice from someone who teaches managers how to fire employees? You should take it because I'm the most qualified person to give it. You need to understand exactly what your company wants from you in order to get what you want from your company. Professional football players and coaches study films and videos of their opponents to learn how to win. Military strategists study their enemies to learn how to win. Attorneys have an old saying, "If you can't beat 'em, hire 'em!" You've hired me to help you learn what you need to know to win at your job and in your career.

There's usually only one most valuable player (MVP) in sports. Mention "Superbowl MVP" to a football fan and listen as he or she rattles off the names of great warriors such as Terry Bradshaw, Joe Montana, or Troy Aikman. The same happens in business. In *Good to Great*,[3] Jim Collins explained how companies such as Walgreen's slaughtered their competition and came to dominate their industry.

Becoming indispensable to your employer is different in three ways:

1. You don't have to compete with anyone other than yourself.
2. You don't have to achieve greatness.
3. There's no limit to how many indispensable employees a company can have.

My research for this book came from three primary sources: First, I spent countless hours talking to the managers who've attended my seminars. Second, I sent surveys to over 7,000 companies, nonprofit agencies, and government institutions, asking what makes an employee indispensable. Their responses are included throughout the book. Third, I interviewed individuals in various jobs. Some of them have sought career coaching from me while I encountered others as a customer. I found 18 qualities to be critical in order for an employee to be indispensable.

Congratulations on taking the first step toward what could easily be the biggest and best move of your career. Now take the second step by reading this book cover to cover. And here's a million dollar tip to help you get the absolute greatest results: Don't read this book in one sitting and don't read it on the weekend. Get up 30 minutes earlier than normal for the next 18 workdays of your life and read one chapter per day while you're still fresh. Then think about what you read on the way to work and implement it that day. Now, let's get to work on making you indispensable to your employer!

Acknowledgments

The most difficult part of writing a book is writing the acknowledgments. It's the last part an author writes and also the most emotional. It symbolizes the end of a project that has consumed every waking minute of every day, and even some sleeping minutes, for months. It also means the onset of a kind of postpartum separation anxiety, and it's at this point that authors are reminded of how many people contributed in so many ways. I thank the following people for helping to make this book happen. Some played large parts while others made minor contributions. Some were actively involved each step of the way, while I've never even met others. Yet, even those I've never met played such a significant part in shaping my thinking and keeping me motivated that it would be a sin not to include them. Words cannot express my gratitude to you all.

First, a very special thanks to my own highly valued employees who remain nameless at their own request. They live and breathe everything I teach in this book and make being the boss a pleasure.

Thanks to Alvin Law in Canada for his story; to Arielle Ford in California for her story; to Brendan Keegan of Marriott International in Washington, DC, for his time and input; to Brian Frasier of Ergonomic Concepts in North Carolina for his time, input, and 25 years of friendship; to Carolyn Ingraham of Augusta State University for her story; and to Cheryl Callighan of EOffice-Virtual Assistants in Colorado for her professionalism, promptness, and incredible skill at deciphering and transposing my "random thought eruptions" from audio into Microsoft Word.

To Colleen C. Barrett, president of Southwest Airlines, for her time, input, and colorful details. You could be a writer in your next career, Colleen. To fellow Nashville resident Dave Ramsey for his daily affirmation that there's a great place to go when people are broke, and it's called "work"; to Dottie Clancy of Courier Printing in Tennessee for her input; to Eddie Brittain of Cherokee Church in Tennessee for his inspiration; to Janice Spencer of Georgia College & State University for her inspiration; to Jim Ziegler of Ziegler Dynamics in Atlanta for his input; to fellow Nashville resident Joe Calloway for his mentoring and the best white chocolate soup at his restaurant Mirror, which is now the official spot for all my book release parties; to John Kremer of Open Horizons in Iowa for his time and suggestions; to John. C. Maxwell of Atlanta for providing so much inspiration in this book, my career, and my life. You are literally God's gift to leadership, John.

Another very special thanks to my executive editor Matthew Holt at Wiley, who first suggested this project. To Kate Lindsay, senior editorial assistant at Wiley, for keeping things flowing between Hoboken and Nashville; to Kevin Holm, senior production editor at Wiley, for doing the toughest job of all; to Nancy Land and Pam Blackmon of Publications Development Company of Texas for making me look smarter than I really am.

Thanks to my friend and colleague Kent Hutchison of C. J. Baxter Group in Texas for everything; to Linda Rutherford, director of public relations at Southwest Airlines, for her time and correspondence among what must be millions of requests; to Dr. Michelle May of Arizona for her time and input; to Michelle Reda of Arby's in Tennessee for her perfect demonstration of how highly valued employees act; and to Mike Telesca of the North Carolina Office of State Personnel for being such a highly valued employee and the most efficient government employee in the world; to Nancy Persson at Staples' world headquarters in Massachusetts for her time and input; to fellow Nashville resident Nat Johnson of the Tennessee Department of Personnel for his time and input; and to Pat Miles at the University of South Alabama for 11 years of loyalty and support.

To Paul Harvey in Chicago for being my personal role model for work. I can only hope that in another 40 years, I'll have half the energy, enthusiasm, and wit Mr. Harvey has today. To Rick Warren in California for his inspiration; to Robin Flynn in Ohio for her story; to T. D. Jakes in Dallas for his inspiration; to Tonya Hurston in Georgia for her story; to Thomas H. Wright of the North Carolina Office of State Personnel for his time and input; and to Tom Stanley and William Danko for revealing the truth about working hard and becoming successful in *The Millionaire Next Door*.

Finally, I must thank all the people who responded to my surveys and attend my seminars. I regret that I couldn't include every response in the book, and I hope this book reflects how much I appreciate all your feedback.

Contents

CONTENTS

CHAPTER 1

First, Understand Why You Need to Be Indispensable

The victory of success will be half won when you learn the secret of putting out more than is expected in all that you do. Make yourself so valuable in your work that eventually you will become indispensable.

Og Mandino

The first step toward becoming indispensable is to understand what the word *indispensable* means and why it is so important to your career. One definition of indispensable is "absolutely necessary." This is not the definition used in this book. I constantly remind managers that everyone is expendable, including themselves. No one individual employee is absolutely necessary for a company to survive. It would not be much of a company if that were the case. A real company must be able to survive even after losing key employees at the highest level. Most people hardly notice when even the most charismatic leaders and talented managers leave their posts. Rudy Giuliani was so adored by the residents of New York City that they tried to change the law so that he could remain mayor for a third term. Even though Mayor Giuliani's successor did not have Giuliani's charisma, the lives of most New York City residents went on as usual after Giuliani's departure. The same thing happened when Jack Welch retired from General Electric (GE). He is a living legend among managers. People who hear him speak at conferences and conventions treat him like a rock star. Yet life went on as usual for most GE customers and employees after his retirement in 2001.

Another definition of indispensable is "essential," which means something is of the highest importance for achieving a specific goal. This is the definition we used in this book. The purpose of this book is to help you become of the highest importance in your company's achievement of excellence. Your company won't value employees regardless of their caliber if it is content being mediocre. A company needs employees of the highest caliber if it wishes to excel.

Contrary to reports, there's no shortage of labor in the United States today. There are over 225 million people currently in the workforce and over 7 million who are looking for a job. I've never met an employer who advertised a job opening in the newspaper and got no response. The quantity of job applicants isn't the problem; it's the quality. I meet over 10,000 managers every year who are frustrated to the point of hopelessness with the declining quality of the labor pool. There's little doubt that our work ethic is deteriorating. This outlook may be bleak for employers but it presents an incredible opportunity for you. The demand for good employees goes up as the supply goes down. This places you in control of your own destiny.

> I want the company to succeed. To do that, we need to get the best people. And if the best people are outside Ford, we will go after them. Or we'll grow them up from inside.
>
> Bill Ford Jr., CEO, Ford Motor Company

Companies Don't Need Employees; They Need *Good* Employees

Payroll is the biggest single expense for most companies. This makes employees their biggest investment, which is why the personnel department has now become the *human resources* department. No business can survive if it doesn't get a good rate of return on its biggest investment.

Although there is no one single employee companies can't live without, there is a category of employees companies can't live without if they are to excel. You must become part of that category if you wish to be indispensable. Being a good employee doesn't make you indispensable; it only makes you valuable. Companies need good employees but hope and pray for indispensable employees. You must be better than good in order to be considered indispensable. This doesn't mean you have to be extraordinary; few of us are. I divide employees into three categories: the highly valued employee, the run-of-the-mill employee, and the lowly valued employee. You must become a highly valued employee if you wish to become indispensable.

Begin by making an honest assessment of your situation. Ask yourself if you're presently a highly valued employee, run-of-the-mill employee, or lowly valued employee. Be brutally honest when you answer this question. If you're not already a highly valued employee, your journey to becoming one begins now. If you're already a highly valued employee, this book will help you maintain that status and become even more valuable.

> The kind of people I look for . . . are the guys who try to do more than they're expected to do.
>
> Lee Iacocca

There's No Such Thing as Job Security

Detective J. J. Bittenbinder spent 23 years with the Chicago Police Department and is widely respected as one of America's leading authorities on personal safety. He teaches people that they can't prevent being the victim of a violent crime. What they can do is make themselves a less attractive target. Detective Bittenbinder teaches people to make themselves the last target a criminal would choose. This is the approach you must take to job security. You can't prevent your company from shutting down or laying you off, but you can make yourself one of the last employees your company would choose to let go. This ensures that you will always have a job as long as your company has a position you're capable of filling. While at GE, Jack Welch was a huge proponent of an employee performance evaluation system called *forced rankings*. This method systematically eliminates employees who are ranked in the bottom 10 percent. Similar systems have been used by Ford, Goodyear, and EDS. The percentage of employees ranked in the bottom or elimination category varies by company. What doesn't vary is that keeping yourself in the top category is the surest way to keep your job. Don't look to your employer for job security because no company can give this to you. You must create your own job security by making yourself a highly valued employee.

> The biggest mistake that you can make is to believe that you're working for somebody else. Job security is gone. The driving force of a career must come from the individual. Remember: Jobs are owned by the company, you own your career.
>
> Earl Nightingale

Money Is Not the Root of All Evil

The first step toward becoming a highly valued employee is clarifying your purpose for working in the first place. It sounds obvious but some people have trouble with this. The vast majority of us work for money. People often say that money is the root of all evil, believing that they are quoting the Bible. This is an inaccurate quote and it's also untrue. The Bible says that *the love of money* is the root of all evil.[1] It's how we handle money that can cause problems. Disagreement over money causes more marital problems than religion, in-laws, or infidelity.

We need money and there's nothing wrong with being well paid for a job well done. Billy Graham's salary was reported at $174,000 for the year 2000. The first official salary for a president of the United States was $25,000 a year in 1789. George Washington declined to accept it even though it was an enormous sum at the time. Bill Clinton's presidential salary was $200,000 a year when he left office in January 2001. George W. Bush began at a salary of $400,000 a year when he took office that same month. Few would argue that each of these men earned every penny they were paid and then some. Bill Gates has given away nearly $30 billion through the Bill and Melinda Gates Foundation. I challenge anyone who thinks that money is evil to tell it to the thousands of children whose lives have been saved because of the medical treatments made possible through the Gates' philanthropy.

I also challenge anyone who thinks that money is evil to try living without it. Money is neither good nor bad. It is simply a necessity. Most of what you'll ever want to do requires money. Whether it's sending your kids to college, feeding the homeless, or buying a new Jaguar convertible, you need money to do it.

Even those who work for a higher calling agree that having more money frees them up to do more of what matters most. Larry King interviewed Rick Warren and asked how money has changed his life. Pastor Warren's book *The Purpose Driven Life*[2] has now sold an estimated 20 million copies and made him one very wealthy pastor. It still didn't change his life very much. He remained in the same house, kept driving the same car, repaid his salary for the past 20 years to his church, and now gives away 90 percent of his income. He continues to pastor at Saddleback Church in Lake Forest, California, but with one minor change. He now works for free. He explained that the money didn't change his life but made it possible for him to change thousands of other people's lives.

Wanting to make the most out of the 40 hours or more you put into work every week doesn't make you greedy, materialistic, or selfish. It makes you wise. If you've got to work, why not make it count? There's nothing wrong with wanting to stay where you are if you're content and able to meet your financial obligations. There's also nothing inherently wrong with wanting to make more money.

If you ask me to name the proudest distinction of Americans, I would choose . . . the fact that they were the people who created the phrase "to make money." No other language or nation had ever used these words before. . . . Americans were the first to understand that wealth has to be created.

Ayn Rand, Author of *Atlas Shrugged*[3]

Conclusion

The first step to becoming indispensable is understanding *why* you need to be indispensable. Becoming indispensable to your employer is the only way to achieve job security. It is also the only way to advance. Making more money is a perfectly acceptable reason to strive to be a highly valued employee because:

- Everyone needs money.
- The surest way to get money is to work.
- The surest way to get more money is to become more valuable at work.

CHAPTER 2

Learn What Your Boss Wants from You

A good employee needs to be smart and savvy to understand the task at hand, as well as, know how to approach work while keeping the temperament and personality of the boss in mind.

Greg Muilenburg, Project Engineer,
CDI Engineering Solutions,
Cincinnati, Ohio

I stated earlier that you need to understand exactly what your company wants from you. You also need to understand exactly what your immediate supervisor expects of you. Mel Gibson developed a psychic ability to read women's minds in the 2000 movie *What Women Want*. This allowed him to get ahead in his job at an advertising agency. I often remind managers that employees aren't mind readers like Gibson was in that movie, and that frontline supervisors are responsible for clearly explaining to their employees what they expect of them. You're also responsible for making sure you know what your supervisor expects of you. If he or she has failed to tell you and you don't have psychic ability, then ask. This opens the channels of communication. Ensure that they remain open in the future by asking for the following:

- A job description
- Regular performance evaluations
- A short, informal meeting with your supervisor each month (this can even be done over lunch)

Even though each of these items is normally as welcome as a root canal, they're as necessary for your career health as a root canal may be for your dental health. You may find that your supervisor isn't even clear on what he or she expects of you. It will be impossible for you to be viewed as a highly valued employee if this is the case. Your value to your organization can't be measured until there's a measuring stick.

> If there's something to gain and nothing to lose by asking, by all means ask!
>
> W. Clement Stone

Stephen Covey's fifth habit of highly effective people is seeking to understand the other person before expecting him to understand you. Nowhere is this more important than in the relationship between you and your supervisor. Sometimes the problem isn't lack of communication; it's miscommunication. This often occurs when your supervisor has a different value system than yours. This is likely if there's a significant age difference between you and your supervisor. Four generations make up most of today's active workforce. It's highly advantageous to know which generation you and your supervisor belong to and to understand the different values of each.

Group 1: The Silent Generation

Members of the Silent Generation were born between 1925 and 1944. They number nearly 50 million. Early members are mostly out of the workforce now and the later members are rapidly reaching retirement age. This generation valued conformity, delay of gratification, discipline, duty, loyalty, and sacrifice. Their value of conformity was exhibited in their respect of the term "company man." Their value of duty and sacrifice was demonstrated by the thousands of men who volunteered to fight World War II and who faced death on D-Day and in the Normandy invasion. Steven Spielberg and Tom Hanks paid homage to this generation in the 1998 movie *Saving Private Ryan*. This sense of duty was also seen in the civilian workforce during the war. Women stepped in to fill the positions left vacant at shipyards and factories when men went off to fight the war. *Rosie the Riveter* became the icon for these women.

Loyalty to employers was expected as was loyalty to employees. The Silent Generation expected to stay in one job for a lifetime. Their value of loyalty can also be seen in their personal lives. They expected to stay in one marriage for a lifetime. Divorce carried such a stigma that political candidates stood little chance of serious consideration for higher office if they were divorced. This generation's value of delayed gratification and discipline was exhibited in their reluctance to borrow money. They saved until they could afford to buy things. Many members of this generation grew up with parents who lived through the Great Depression and consequently were financially disciplined. It's easy to understand why the Silent Generation is also called the Greatest Generation. Their exit from the workforce is a great loss for everyone.

Group 2: The Baby Boomers

The Baby Boomers were born between 1946 and 1964. They number approximately 75 million. They were very optimistic, upbeat, and celebrated life. They were also narcissistic and self-absorbed. The first wave of Baby Boomers made each life stage trendy as soon as they hit it. When Baby Boomers first began hitting their thirties, magazines ran stories with titles such as "Still Sexy at 30." A decade later it was "Still Hot at 40," followed by "Still Beautiful at 50," and "Still Sassy at 60."

Their fashion choices reveal much about their attitudes. They wore flowers in their hair, bell-bottom jeans, and wide belts to be "groovy" in the 1960s. They wore leisure suits to be "hip" in the 1970s. This image was captured in Steve Martin and Dan Akroyd's "Two Wild and Crazy Guys" from *Saturday Night Live*. Guys slicked back their hair and put on bright fluorescent colors to be "cool" like Don Johnson on *Miami Vice* in the mid-1980s. They wore pink button-down shirts and pinstripe suits to the office. This launched the era of the yuppies (young urban professionals). Women also put on pinstripes for the office. Their casual wear was tights and t-shirts with cut-out collars falling off their shoulders to mimic Jennifer Beals from the movie *Flashdance*. Perms and big hair became all the rage by the late 1980s. Glitzy musicians such as Motley Crue and Bon Jovi dressed in bright leather, spandex, and makeup, helping spawn the phrase "The Big Eighties." Their focus on dressing well was captured by the ZZ Top song "Sharp Dressed Man" and John T. Malloy's book *Dress for Success*.[1]

Baby Boomers' values were also reflected in their music. The optimism of the 1960s can be heard in songs such as "The Age of Aquarius," which celebrated harmony and understanding. Their upbeat, happy attitude can be heard in 1970s songs from groups such as ABBA, KC and the Sunshine Band, and the Bee Gees. This music became a target of ridicule for a while and then made a comeback in some unusual places. Listen closely the next time you're in a Wal-Mart or Applebee's. You'll hear 1970s music playing and see people silently singing along or tapping a toe. These retail establishments are playing this music because it appeals to the age group they're targeting, but there's more to it. Marketing professionals know that people buy more when they're in a good mood. Happy music works on customers of every age. Look closely and you'll notice that even teenagers are lip-syncing to the music of the Bee Gees even though they'd never listen to it on the radio or admit they like it.

The 1980s were called "The Age of Conspicuous Consumption" and Baby Boomers were extremely good at consuming. Their motto was "Live now, pay later." Home mortgage rates topped 18 percent and debt became a way of life. Preapproved credit card offers began to appear in mailboxes everywhere and automobile leasing became common. The status symbols were convertible BMWs, gold serpentine necklaces for men, and a new gadget called a cellular phone. Baby Boomers were so vain that those who couldn't afford a $750 cell phone bought fake cell phone antennas for their cars. (I must confess that I was one of those vain young Baby Boomers who did this in 1987.)

Baby Boomers were hard working. Earlier members of this generation were largely responsible for the civil rights movements of the 1960s. They had a social conscience and took action that changed the social landscape of our country. Later members placed a higher value on material wealth and status but also valued the career success necessary to finance materialistic desires. They considered working long hours a virtue. Movies such as *Wall Street* with Michael Douglas, *Working Girl* with Melanie Griffith, and *An Officer and a Gentleman* with Richard Gere revealed how much Baby Boomers respected those who worked hard to succeed.

Lifetime employment with the same company was no longer expected, but there was still some sense of loyalty between employer and employee. It was generally considered inappropriate to stay at a job less than two years. Employees were expected to offer a two-week notice when they tendered resignations.

Divorce became socially acceptable for Baby Boomers. This change was reflected in politics when Ronald Reagan became the first divorced man to be elected president in 1980. Baby Boomers were also largely viewed as power hungry.

Group 3: Generation X

Generation X were born between 1965 and 1981. It's the smallest generation alive today at an estimated 19 million. It's sometimes referred to as the "lost generation" because of its association with having an identity crisis. GenXers are extremely nonconformist. They rebelled against most of the values of the Baby Boomers. They didn't want to climb the company ladder like the Baby Boomers. Generation X distrusted big corporations and became highly entrepreneurial. Part of this came from the changing job market. Many GenXers found themselves graduating college and unable to find a job. They took temporary jobs in fast-food restaurants to get by until they found permanent employment. This trend was so common that the term "McJobs" became a catch phrase for the generation.

Their fashion trend was a backlash to the glam and glitter Baby Boomers wore in the 1980s. In stark contrast to the Baby Boomers who dressed up in bright colors, Generation X dressed down in dark grunge colors. They flocked to stores to buy flannel shirts and Doc Martin boots or Converse sneakers. Perms and big hair were replaced with straight and stringy hair.

Their music also reflected this change in attitude. Generation X music was characterized by cynicism and angst. Grunge rock bands like Nirvana launched this era in 1991 when they sang about feeling stupid and contagious in "Smells Like Teen Spirit." Beck suggested that someone just kill him in his 1994 song "Loser." Alanis Morissette whined about being underpaid, tired, and sick in her 1995 song "Hand in My Pocket." In contrast to Baby Boomers' hunger for power, Generation X is often associated with powerlessness. Politicians exacerbated this powerlessness by proclaiming Generation X was the first generation that didn't expect to do better than their parents. The optimism of the Baby Boomers was replaced with the pessimism of Generation X. Some historians have attributed the beginning of our country's obsession with being a victim to this shift in attitude.

Generation X distrusts institutions and feels little loyalty to employers. They see themselves as free agents in the job market and consider it acceptable to change jobs more frequently than previous generations. They're bigger risk takers who place less value on security than previous generations did. This willingness to take risks accounted for much of the dot-com revolution of the 1990s. Generation X values were also reflected in the way they ran their companies. They believed work should be fun and heralded in an age when employees could dress any way they wanted, bring their dogs to work, and set their own hours.

GenXers became a little more conformist when the dot-coms collapsed in 2000 and thousands of people lost their jobs. The new high-tech companies that survived began hiring corporate Baby Boomers they called "suits" to help run their companies.

Group 4: Generation Next

Generation Next was born starting around 1982. No real consensus on the ending year will be reached until the next generation is named. It will probably be set somewhere around the year 2000. This generation is also known as Generation Y, the Millenials, and Echo Boomers. Their parents are mostly Baby Boomers. Nexters are nearly 80 million strong and are just entering the workforce. Nexters aren't rebellious and independent like Generation X. They're highly conformist and have a very strong groupthink mentality. They don't want to stand out; they want to fit in. Social benefits of this shift in values have been decreases in teenage crime, smoking, and pregnancy. They're also the most inclusive and tolerant generation ever. This increased tolerance has resulted in a decrease in social problems such as racism.

Their music has elements from both of the previous two generations. The happy music of the Baby Boomers is reflected in Generation Next's stars such as Brittany Spears and Jessica Simpson. The angry music of Generation X is reflected in gangster rap.

Their fashion trends also have elements from both of the previous two generations. They don't dress up like Baby Boomers but are more fashion conscious than Generation X. The Nexters' fashion choices include low-rise jeans, tattoos, and the piercing of multiple body parts.

The education system placed such a high value on self-esteem in the 1990s that Generation Next has grown up with what psychologists call a "false sense of self." They've also been referred to as the Trophy Generation because they received trophies for everything. Kids who came in first, second, or third place won trophies. So did the kids who came in ninth, tenth, and last place. Teachers were told to discontinue using red ink to correct student's homework because it hurt the children's feelings. My hometown of Nashville abolished the honor role so those who didn't make it wouldn't feel left out. Charles Sykes summarized this in *Dumbing Down Our*

Kids: Why American Children Feel Good About Themselves But Can't Read, Write, or Add.[2]

Parents also contributed to this generation's false sense of self. We went from an era when Bill Cosby joked about how kids cause parents to lose their sanity in his 1986 book *Fatherhood*[3] to an era when parents idolized their children to the point of obsession. Yellow "Baby-on-Board" signs appeared in minivan windows everywhere in the 1980s. Now minivan and SUV owners plaster their windows with stickers advertising that their child is an honor student, on a sports team, or a cheerleader. Baby Boomers who held material possessions as their status symbols in the 1980s have now turned their children into status symbols by living vicariously through them. Keeping up with the Joneses has turned into keeping their kids up with the Joneses' kids. This obsession with competitive parenting escalated to the point of a Texas mother[4] attempting to kill a competing child and her mother in order for her daughter to make the cheerleading team, and a Massachusetts father[5] beating another father to death when his 10-year-old son got too rough in a hockey game.

Nexters' lives were heavily programmed by what psychologists call "helicopter parents" who constantly hovered over them. Nexters were driven to so many after-school activities that their parents often referred to the days of the week by the kid's activities: Monday was soccer day, Tuesday was Scout day, and so on. Members of Generation Next aren't risk takers like their predecessors. Most have never ridden in a car without a seatbelt and airbags, ridden a skateboard without kneepads, or a bicycle without a helmet.

Nexters are highly materialistic and are accustomed to getting what they want. This was made possible because of the better economic times they grew up in as well as technology. Nexters' parents had greater affluence than previous generations. Mortgage interest rates dropped to 5 percent and interest rates for automobiles dropped to 0 percent. Parents of Nexters began buying homes that would be considered mansions by standards of previous generations and driving $70,000 SUVs. They denied themselves nothing and denied their children nothing. These overindulgent parents bought their children $200 tennis shoes, name brand clothing, and $300

MP3 players. In just two generations, we went from teenage Baby Boomers begging for a phone or television in their rooms to Generation Next where every teenager has a cell phone and every family vehicle has a DVD player in the back.

Nexters also expect immediate gratification and are used to getting it. Instead of shopping at the mall, they shop online and have whatever they order overnighted by FedEx. They're more accustomed to downloading their favorite songs off the Internet than buying a CD.

How to Work with the Different Generations

Determine which generation you belong to and compare your personal values. You may find that your values more closely reflect those of another generation. This is especially common if you were born on the cusp between two generations. It's not important that you decide which generation you belong to. It's important that you understand your values and how they differ from your boss's values. You must be able to bridge the gap between the two. Let's look at how the different generations work together.

Working for a Silent Generation Boss

Silent generation bosses place a higher value on formality than succeeding generations. This formality can be seen in their fashion trends. They came of age in a time when people dressed up to go to the doctor, get on an airplane, or even go to the grocery store. Work was the most formal destination for many. Casual Fridays were unheard of. This formality in the workplace can also be heard in the way they addressed their bosses. They rarely called the boss by his first name. To have heard Lucille Ball address Mr. Mooney as Theodore would have been scandalous.

If you're a Baby Boomer, GenXer, or Nexter working for a Silent Generation boss, respect his or her appreciation of structure and formality. The relationship will be less personal. They strongly believe in separating work life from home life and don't want to hear about what you did over the weekend. They have better interpersonal skills, greater respect, and more consideration of others than succeeding generations have. They'll be tactful in their dealings with you and will expect the same in return. A good way to show respect to your Silent Generation boss is to ask about his business experiences. This will allow you to learn from his mistakes without having to make the mistakes yourself. It will also show respect for your superior, which is important to Silent Generation bosses.

Working for a Baby Boomer Boss

Baby Boomer bosses can be optimistic to the point of being annoying. They like to be the star of the show and are good at assigning blame to others. They also like to talk about vision and ask about your five-year plan. They like to hold meetings and can come across as controlling. Be prepared for your Baby Boomer boss to micromanage. You can counteract this by taking the initiative to keep him or her in the loop on whatever's going on. I vividly remember my first boss after college in 1985 teaching me the mantra "Out of sight, out of mind, but never out of control."

Baby Boomers see working long hours as a virtue and may see your prompt exit at five o'clock as a lack of commitment. Volunteer to come in early, work late, or come in on the weekends when it's necessary. You'll benefit from time and a half pay if you're an hourly employee. If you're salaried, this will show your boss that you're a team player, which is another big plus with Baby Boomers.

Working for a Generation X Boss

If you're not a GenXer but work for a Generation X boss, the first adjustment you'll have to make is to his directness. He often believes that being brutally honest is best and sometimes lacks interpersonal skills. He's highly independent and self-reliant so he may mistake your team player tendency as a sign of weakness or neediness. He hates meetings and won't be as concerned about your personal development as a Baby Boomer or Silent Generation boss would. He has more of an "every person for him- or herself" outlook. He doesn't value work for the work itself. Staying late or coming in on weekends won't look like a sign of commitment to a Generation X boss. He often prefers that you leave promptly because he likes to leave promptly. Generation X bosses see structure as bureaucracy and are cynical about it. They also dislike labels. (And remember that Generation X bosses will act this way whether male or female. These are general traits shared by men and women.)

Baby Boomers or Generation Xers have already been in the workforce long enough to understand much of this. Employers are reporting that many members of Generation Next are having difficulty adapting to the workplace. If you're a Nexter, you'll have to redefine the values you were taught in school. You'll no longer be rewarded for fitting in. You get rewarded at work for standing out. You'll also have to adapt to your company's values; it's not going to adapt to yours. This may mean removing your facial piercings or dressing in a way you don't like. Nat Johnson, Tennessee's Deputy Commissioner of Personnel summarized it best. He explains to young women who want to bare their midriffs that it's fine to dress this way to fit in to their peer group outside the office. The desire to fit in is normal. This desire is so strong that Dr. Abraham Maslow identified it as the third greatest need of human beings. Nat recommends that young people think of work the same way. They also need to fit in at work and that might mean respecting values that might be different from theirs.

Conclusion

Each generation has strengths and weaknesses. None has been proven to be easier or better to work for, but you'll find it easier to work for a supervisor who shares your values. Learning what your supervisor's values are is critical to becoming a highly valued employee. Start by answering the following questions.

1. I am a member of:
   - The Silent Generation
   - The Baby Boomers
   - Generation X
   - Generation Next

2. My boss is a member of:
    • The Silent Generation
    • The Baby Boomers
    • Generation X
    • Generation Next
3. The values of my boss's generation are: _____
4. Areas in which my values differ from my boss's are: _____
5. Ways I can accommodate my boss's values: _____

CHAPTER 3

Be Low Maintenance

I'd rather have 30 people who do a fair day's work and avoid conflict than 30 of the best, most productive workers who like to stir the pot.

Dennis Sensat, Pioneer Natural
Resources, Irving, Texas

Have you ever worked around people who just suck the life out of you? You feel drained at the end of the day. No matter how good they are at their job, working around them seems to make your job that much harder. It doesn't even have to be performance related. Managers constantly tell me that just a little bad behavior can completely override all the productivity in the world.

Sometimes it's not even behavior, but just certain mannerisms that tire you out. Trying to do something as simple as holding a conversation with some people can be draining. Maybe she's a Chatty Cathy type who won't let you get a word in edgewise. Maybe he's the long-winded type who tells you how to build a clock when you only asked for the time.

You can't change other people's mannerisms, but you can change your own. Most of us are aware of our personal quirks. It's much harder to see our "work quirks," and these are the ones that matter most.

Be Flexible Enough to Adapt to Change

One of the most insurmountable hurdles for employers is trying to manage employees who fight change. Change is inevitable in business. Those who embrace change prosper while those who don't struggle throughout their careers. This is true because things don't always go as well as planned in business. In fact, plans seldom go off without a hitch. An engineer working at Edwards Air Force Base in 1949 formed a theory on this that became legend. Captain Edward Murphy got so angry with a technician for wiring a transducer wrong that he is reported to have said, "If there's any way to do it wrong, he'll find it." Aerospace manufacturers began quoting his famous words and Murphy's Law evolved into "Whatever can go wrong, will go wrong." While it was actually based on a much older English saying called Sod's Law, the underlying premise is the same. Even the best-laid plans can fall apart on a moment's notice. Companies and their employees must be able to adapt quickly.

> Be open to change even when something is frightening. Show that you will try.
>
> Kay Spillers, Clinic Manager, Willis-Knighton
> Health System, Shreveport, Louisiana

History is rich with examples of careers that were instantly launched or abruptly ended because of sudden changes in the marketplace. Al Capone was already in prison when prohibition was repealed in 1933. Had he still been making a fortune as a bootlegger, he would have been out of a job overnight. Future president John F. Kennedy's father Joseph immediately began legally importing alcohol and making millions. A single change in the law ended one career and launched another.

A half century later in the 1980s, the personal computer industry exploded. Compaq quickly emerged as an industry leader by becoming the first to successfully clone the IBM PC. They filled the shelves of retail stores such as Sears and Circuit City. They built a retail distribution network most companies only dream of and seemed unstoppable. Meanwhile, a college student who began building computers in his dorm room at the University of Texas in 1984 was coming on strong with no retail outlets. He was able to sell computers cheaper by eliminating the middleman and selling directly via telephone. He kept his inventory costs next to nothing by only building computers after they were ordered. His company then rode a new wave called the Internet and Dell Computer became the largest personal computer company in the world. Michael Dell also became one of the wealthiest men in the world by adapting to change faster and better than his competitors. This ability became critical as computer technology continued to change on nearly a daily basis. Companies like Compaq tried to emulate Dell's system but were unsuccessful because they were too entrenched in their existing structure to make the change.

The personal computer industry was still in its infancy when Michael Dell brought about such a drastic change. A much slower transition happened in the pizza industry. Brothers Dan and Frank Carney opened the first Pizza Hut in Wichita, Kansas, in 1958 after borrowing $600 from their mother. They chose the name because they wanted "pizza" in it and there was only room for three more letters on the sign. They believed the key to their success would be their highly valued employees and they were right. Their company quickly came to dominate the pizza parlor business. By 1980, Pizza Hut had opened its four thousandth store.

Brothers Tom and Nick Monaghan borrowed $500 to buy a pizza store named "Dominick's" in Ypsilanti, Michigan, in 1960. That company became Domino's. It wasn't until 1967 that Domino's opened its first franchise store, nearly a decade after the first Pizza Hut opened. They opened their two hundredth store in 1978, their thousandth store in 1983, and their five thousandth store in 1989.

To add to the fray, John Schnatter started making pizza in a broom closet at his father's pub in a suburb of Louisville, Kentucky, in 1984. He sold his 1972 Camaro Z-28 to buy $1,600 worth of equipment and launched Papa John's. Today they have nearly 3,000 locations.

Pizza Hut saw its early market dominance eroded by later arriving competition and a drastic shift in how people bought pizza. Pizza had suddenly gone from an eat-in restaurant experience to mostly carry-out to mostly home delivery. Pizza Hut remained competitive because they adjusted to the shift in the way their industry functioned.

> Change can be scary. Change can be unsettling. And, certainly, not all change is good. But change, when undertaken for the right reasons, is very healthy.
>
> Gary Cowger, President, General Motors
> North America, Detroit, Michigan

Think Things Through to the Logical Conclusion

Managers find people who are mentally lazy extremely annoying. A manager in Illinois compared this to someone who, when you take him to lunch, wants you to cut up his food for him. It's as if these people begin a thought, then get tired of thinking about it, and expect someone else to finish their thought process. If you work with people like this, you'll have a tendency to avoid being on committees or in work groups with them because you know their presence will mean more of a burden for you. You'll feel like you can never let your guard down around them because they don't think things through to the logical conclusion. They may have good intentions and want to help, but you'll become so conditioned to them not thinking their ideas through that you almost wish they wouldn't make any more suggestions. A manager in Florida compared it to getting a dog for her 6-year-old son. She knew he'd love the dog and be good to it. She also knew she'd end up being the one who fed it.

Imagine that you work in a law office where Barbara is your coworker. Your copy machine is on its last leg. You and Barbara have been appointed to research new copiers and make a recommendation to the partners. Bids from the first three vendors each come in around $20,000. Barbara continues shopping until she finds a comparable machine for only $15,000. The machine's manufacturer has an excellent record for reliability and other law firms report it to be nearly maintenance free. Barbara is about to turn in the proposals to the partners when you ask her what the operating costs are. She tells you the other firms reported it to have virtually no maintenance costs. Barbara was so enthusiastic about saving the $5,000 that she didn't think things through. You explain that maintenance costs include only repairs and routine service, but operating costs include maintenance costs plus the cost of supplies. You review the paperwork and discover the $15,000 machine has a toner cost of two cents per copy while the others have a toner cost of one cent per copy. Barbara still doesn't see how a one-penny difference could matter when the machine costs $5,000 less. You point out that your firm makes over one million copies per year. The difference in the annual cost will be over $10,000. This would be an additional $100,000 over the next 10 years. She sincerely thanks you for saving her from embarrassment and drops the $15,000 machine from consideration. You wish she had just stayed out of it.

This would have been no big deal if it was an isolated incident, but it wasn't. It was typical of Barbara. She always takes initiative to do what needs to be done and adapts well to change. She also wastes resources of her coworkers and managers by failing to think things through to the logical conclusion. Barbara is a high-maintenance employee.

Failing to think things through can have an immediate personal financial impact on some workers. I once paid a server at a Kansas City restaurant a $19.95 tab with a $100 bill. She brought back my change in a black leather folder and walked away. I opened it to find four $20 bills and a nickel. I didn't have any smaller bills and her service was far from being worth a $20 tip. I tried to call her back to get change but could never get her attention. I finally decided that she would get what she deserved if she was that mentally lazy. I placed the nickel in the leather folder and left.

Don't Cherry-Pick the Pleasant Tasks

Another work quirk that frustrates managers is the employee who excels at his duties but only does those he enjoys while leaving the less desirable tasks for someone else. A manager in Virginia compared this to a family member who takes all the big potato chips out of the bag and leaves the crumbs for everyone else.

A similar problem sometimes happens with parents of young children. She might be a responsible mother who disciplines her children when necessary while he is an irresponsible father who would rather play with his kids than discipline them. He always gets to be the good cop while she has to be the bad cop. Being the only disciplinarian is more work for her. It's hurtful to hear her child say, "Why are you so mean to me Mommy? Daddy never makes me clean up my room." The parent who never disciplines a child is doing serious damage to the child's development. This wisdom goes back long before Dr. Laura and Dr. Phil. Proverbs says that parents who don't discipline their kids prove they don't love them and that it will ruin their lives.[1] Yet, she'll resent being made out to be the bad cop no matter how vindicated her actions may be. Ask parents who've been in this position and they'll tell you that it feels like having an additional child instead of having a partner in the marriage.

Now let's apply this to the workplace. A factory foreman in Pennsylvania told me how his employees suffered financially when others didn't carry their duties out all the way. He supervised the day shift and his employees had to spend 15 minutes each morning cleaning up the mess left by the night shift. They also spent 15 minutes each afternoon cleaning up their own mess. They were losing a half hour of production each day. This allowed the night shift to post higher production numbers. Bonuses were paid to the most productive team and always went to the night shift. His employees were being penalized for doing their jobs thoroughly. Once a new plant manager came in and began holding the night shift accountable for cleaning up, the day shift began exceeding the night shift's production and earning the bonuses.

You won't be a highly valued employee unless you do the entire job. This includes the unpleasant parts such as filing, filling out paperwork, or cleaning up. Such tasks may seem unimportant but they're still part of your job.

Highly Productive People Can Still Be High Maintenance

People can excel at what they do and still be high maintenance. This applies to all aspects of life. A minister in Kentucky told me about a member of his congregation whose faithful giving accounted for nearly 20 percent of the church's annual income. Yet this parishioner took so much of the minister's time with his "helpful" suggestions that he was considering asking the parishioner to join another church.

I once heard a caller to a radio talk show complain that her husband accused her of being high maintenance. She claimed she couldn't be high maintenance because she was the most unselfish person she knew. The host explained that being unselfish is a separate issue from being low maintenance and that the two can have an inverse relationship. Selfish people can actually be more low maintenance than unselfish people. The host used the example of a wife whose husband always forgets her birthday. She won't be happy about his forgetfulness but it does provide an odd benefit. She won't be expected to do much for him on his birthday. She can just give him a card and feel like a more thoughtful person than him.

There would be higher expectations of her if she were married to a more thoughtful man. Imagine that he served her a candlelit dinner for her birthday. He then surprised her with a hot bubble bath complete with rose petals, champagne, and chocolate. This Harlequin romance night might be a dream come true for some women, but it might be more like a bad dream when his birthday rolls around. She'll feel obligated to do more for him and may not want to work that hard. She may wish he had just taken her to dinner at her favorite restaurant on her birthday so she could do the same for him on his. He's definitely not selfish. He's also not low maintenance.

Now let's apply this to the workplace. An employee's high level of productivity becomes less valuable if he or she takes up too much of the company's resources. I learned this at my first job after college. I was a management trainee who did everything I was asked to do, took initiative to do what needed to be done without being asked, and put in long hours. I also walked into my general manager's office every time his door was open and updated him on what was going on. One day he tactfully suggested that I make a list of things I needed to tell him and save it for one meeting at the end of the day. I can now see what a pest I was running into his office every hour to say "Look at me! Didn't I do well?" I didn't see it then because I had never been in his position. My enthusiasm was consuming too much of my boss's time and making me a high-maintenance employee.

I didn't understand this for four reasons. First, my thinking was very short term. Ten minutes was only 10 minutes to me. I never stopped long enough to realize that if I occupied 10 minutes of my boss's time six times a day, I took an hour out of his time. Second, I never considered that I was one of many employees wanting his time. He couldn't afford to give 10 minutes a day to every employee and certainly not an hour. Third, I didn't appreciate the difference in our life stages. I was 21 and single. I didn't mind working late because I had nowhere else to be. He had a wife and kids waiting to see him, and he didn't want to add an hour to his day by shooting the breeze with me. Fourth, I didn't take into consideration that his salary was about twice what mine was. Ten minutes of his time cost the same as 20 minutes of mine. His time was more expensive and I needed to understand that.

Conclusion

Being a highly productive employee doesn't always translate into being a highly valued employee. To become a highly valued employee, you must be highly productive and low maintenance. Ask your boss if he or she characterizes you as high maintenance or low maintenance. If the answer is high maintenance, ask what you need to do to change that. Also ask your boss what your "work quirks" are.

CHAPTER 4

Answer the Questions Your Boss Didn't Ask

What makes an employee indispensable? He knows his job, everything about the job, all the details, all the background, why the job is done the way it is, the contacts that can get you what you need fast, the time lines to get anything done, how to fill out all the forms, all the weird stuff that doesn't make any sense, answers to the questions that haven't been asked.

Harold R. Brown Jr., HIV/AIDS
Prevention and Control,
Montgomery, Alabama

Stephen Covey's first habit of highly effective people is that of being proactive. This means taking initiative to act before events or circumstances force us into reacting. One danger in reacting is that we act hastily and make bad decisions. Another danger in reacting is that we aren't in control of our circumstances; we let our circumstances control us. Going through life with no control translates into powerlessness.

Few people are truly proactive. Most trudge along one day at a time and never think about the future. Even those who do often say things like "I'm ready for whatever tomorrow might bring." They actually *plan* to react to forces outside of their control instead of taking control of their own destinies. Lowly valued employees make a similar mistake by aimlessly trudging along day after day. They assume they'll just follow whatever career path the company has planned out for them. The problem is that most companies don't have a career path planned out for their employees. In *How to Become CEO,*[1] Jeffrey Fox says this is why people must plan their own career paths.

The best way to affect your career future is by becoming a highly valued employee today. One way to do this is to become so proactive that you answer questions before your boss asks them. Examples of how proactive people become highly valued employees can be seen on television. Gary Burghoff played a highly valued military employee in his role as Radar O'Reilly on *MASH* from 1972 to 1982. He was nicknamed Radar because of his uncanny ability to know about things before they happened. He often had more impact on keeping the camp running than the commanding officer. He became indispensable by doing things such as obtaining the forms needed to get the forms to order more forms.

Michael J. Fox played a highly valued public service employee as New York City Deputy Mayor Michael Flaherty from 1996 to 2000 on *Spin City.* Actor Barry Bostwick's character Mayor Randall Winston couldn't keep the city running for a day without his highly valued deputy mayor.

Actor David Spade played a longer haired and more hip highly valued employee at a women's magazine from 1997 to 2003 in *Just Shoot Me.* The chemistry between each of these employees and his boss was reminiscent of that of a couple that has been married for years.

Burghoff, Fox, and Spade did more than complete their boss's sentences; they completed their bosses. They constantly answered the questions that hadn't been asked, did what needed to be done before their bosses even knew it needed to be done, and thought things through even better than their bosses.

A good employee foresees things that need to be done and will take care of it.

> Carol Odom, Office Manager,
> Oconee Urology, Milledgeville, Georgia

The Most Important Question a Highly Valued Employee Can Ask

Anyone can put himself on the fast track to becoming a highly valued employee by asking his boss one question: "What can I do to help you?" The employee who does this comes out miles ahead of the one who is always willing to help but does so only when asked. See for yourself how well this works by walking into your boss's office and asking, "What can I do to help you?"

This is about more than taking initiative. Taking initiative means doing what needs to be done without being asked to do so. That can only occur when the need has already made itself known. This is about you going to your boss and offering to help before you even know a need exists. A run-of-the-mill employee may accomplish just as much and do just as good of a job as a highly valued employee. Asking the boss how you can help before he asks you makes the distinction between the two.

> If you only do what your boss tells you to do, you haven't done enough.
>
> Jack Welch
> Boston, Massachusetts

Imagine that you're competing against two other contestants for a $1 million grand prize on *Jeopardy*. Host Alex Trebek says, "This is the highest earning rock band in history." You reach for the button but the player next to you hits his first and exclaims, "Who are The Rolling Stones?" You knew the answer but lost $1 million because someone else beat you to the button. Think of your job in the same way and beat your boss to the button.

One benefit of offering to help before you're asked is that you'll still benefit even when there's nothing for you to do. Even when there is work to be done and you end up doing more, the rewards will be substantial over your years with the company. Asking what you can do to help does three things:

1. Gets the job done.
2. Takes one task off your boss's shoulders.
3. Communicates to your boss that you're a highly valued employee.

> A truly good employee exceeds satisfactory performance. You can ask your employee to type a letter and find it satisfactory to receive the letter requested. If you have a truly good employee, you can expect to receive from that same request a grammatically correct letter, envelope with postage, and proper attachments.
>
> Tori Caldwell, Legal Assistant, The Farrar
> Law Firm, Hot Springs, Arkansas

> Always give the boss more than he or she asked for.
>
> Renee Fordyce-Boyer, Laboratory Manager,
> Human Genetics Laboratory, University of Nebraska
> Medical Center, Omaha, Nebraska

Conclusion

Being a highly valued employee requires more than doing the job or volunteering when help is needed. It also requires offering to help before you know help is needed. There are three magic words that can launch a romantic relationship, "I love you"; two that can save a failing relationship, "I'm sorry"; and seven that can immediately define a highly valued employee, "What can I do to help you?" Use those seven magic words with your boss and watch how quickly they work.

CHAPTER 5

Understand the Economic Realities of Employing People

If you're only doing what you're getting paid for, and doing it no better than the average employee, then your pay is most likely right where it should be.

Bo Bennett, Archieboy Holdings, LLC,
Sudbury, Massachusetts

I sometimes hear clerks at retail stores complain, "They don't pay me enough to do this job." They believe that if they were paid more, they'd do a better job. It doesn't occur to them that they're putting the cart before the horse. A person who won't give 100 percent at a job that pays $6 an hour won't give 100 percent at a job that pays $60 an hour. Conversely, the employee who gives 100 percent when making minimum wage won't be making minimum wage very long.

The first principle business professionals learn in marketing is that success will come only when they can answer the question: "What's in it for me?" or WIFM. Every dollar spent, every ounce of brand loyalty ever created, and every purchasing decision ever made was because one company answered the WIFM question better than others.

The second marketing principle lies in the difference between features and benefits. Features are what distinguish one product from another. Benefits are the WIFM that the features provide for the customer. All the features in the world are meaningless unless customers see some benefit to them. Imagine that you're a sales representative at a car dealership. You're trying to sell a used Mercedes Benz to a prospective buyer who asks why he should buy a Mercedes instead of a different luxury car. You enthusiastically explain that the Mercedes has a diesel engine. The buyer could care less. You see the diesel engine as a great feature but the customer sees no WIFM. Next you explain that diesel engines can easily go 200,000 miles without needing a major repair and burn less fuel. The prospect will now be more interested but still won't be sold. Next you explain that the estimated savings would be in excess of $20,000 over 200,000 miles. This is more than the asking price of the car. You've now created enough WIFM to close the deal.

Employers want to know what they're getting for their money just as consumers do. Your employer or prospective employer wants to know what's in it for him, not what's in it for you. Companies don't give a new employee a paycheck on his first day and then hope he'll stick around long enough to earn it. The employee has to earn it first and then be rewarded with a paycheck. He also has to work hard before he gets a raise. He doesn't get a raise first with the promise to work harder later. This is the necessary order of things.

Earn Your Paycheck Every Day

It's crucial that you understand the basic economics of business in order for you to become a highly valued employee. No matter how well managed a company may be, how loyal its customers are, or how hard its employees work, it will cease to exist if it doesn't make a profit. Profit margins in most industries are razor thin. The manager of a New York theatre told me they made only a 75 cent profit on the $7.50 ticket price for a recent *Harry Potter* movie. That 10 percent profit margin is astronomical compared to many industries. General Motors only makes about $400 on the sale of a $40,000 SUV. That's a 1 percent profit margin. The manager of a Tennessee wholesale food supplier once told me he doesn't make a single penny when he unloads a tractor trailer full of his company's products at the Opryland Hotel in Nashville, even though it's his largest customer. Large customers allow the supplier to keep its trucks full so that he can sell to lower volume customers at higher prices.

Large customers demanding deep discounts aren't the only force making it tough to remain profitable in today's business climate. Increased market efficiency and better technologies have made business more competitive than ever. It's cutthroat and it keeps getting more difficult to prosper. Phone companies saw long distance prices plummet from 50 cents per minute to less than 5 cents per minute in the past 30 years. Now cell phone companies and Voice Over Internet Protocol (VOIP) offer long-distance calling for a flat fee. Computer manufacturers have seen personal computer prices plummet from over $2,000 to less than $300 in the past decade. Fax machines that sold for nearly $1,000 just over a decade ago now sell for $50. Cell phones that sold for $400 now sell for less than $20. As prices have dropped, salaries have continued to rise. Payroll remains the biggest single expense for most companies. This is why it's crucial for highly valued employees to be more valuable than others and to earn every dollar they're paid.

> A good employee gives me an honest day's work all day!
>
> Susan Otto, Midwest Thermal Vac,
> Kenosha, Wisconsin

Don't Let Job Seniority Work against You

Unless you work in a unionized company that has a collective bargaining agreement or a government agency with civil service protection, you work under the legal doctrine of employment at will. This means that your employer can fire you at any time without prior notice and without cause. This may sound unfair the first time you hear it, but it's actually the fairest way of doing things. Employment at will protects productive employees by allowing companies to get rid of unproductive employees. Productive employees would have to pick up the slack for unproductive employees if companies were forced to keep poor performers.

Employment at will also allows employers to change the terms of employment at any time. This means your boss could walk in tomorrow and slash your wages by as much as he chooses as long as it doesn't place you below minimum wage. Of course, this rarely happens. A more common example is when companies change health insurance coverage. Thousands of companies have increased employees' co-pay, share of monthly premiums, or dropped benefits such as dental coverage to combat the skyrocketing cost of health insurance. Employers have the legal right to do this without seeking approval of their employees.

Employment at will also creates an obligation for you. You work at your employer's will and must earn your paycheck every day. This doesn't change no matter how long you've been with the company. Some people make the mistake of believing their job becomes more secure the longer they stay with a company. The opposite is actually true from a strictly balance sheet perspective. Your compensation will continue to increase the longer you stay with a company. This is called *salary creep*. Your productivity must also increase to keep up with your salary increases. If your productivity doesn't increase but your cost to your employer does, your value decreases the longer you stay with the company.

Salary creep is most visible in professional sports. The Dallas Cowboys released football legend Emmitt Smith in 2003 after 13 stellar years with the team. He holds the record for the most rushing touchdowns, most rushing attempts, most 1000-yard seasons, and most postseason rushing touchdowns. He played his last two seasons with the Arizona Cardinals before retiring two years later. Dallas adored him so much that they signed him to a ceremonial contract in 2005 that placed him on their reserve list so that he could officially retire from the Cowboys. So why did they let him go if they adored him so much? It obviously wasn't because he didn't produce. It also wasn't because he was high maintenance. He was such a positive role model that he served as a team ambassador when many of his teammates were getting into legal trouble. The Cowboys let him go because his salary crept up so high that he was too expensive to keep.

A similar situation happens in Hollywood. We've become accustomed to actors in popular television series demanding more money and getting whatever they ask for, but this wasn't always the case. Actress Suzanne Somers was fired from the highly successful 1970s show *Three's Company* after demanding more money.

People see this in professional sports and entertainment but sometimes forget that it applies to everyone else. Imagine an employee who is hired at $400 per week and yields $1,000 of productivity per week. His net value to the company is $600 per week. Now let's assume he receives a raise of $50 per week each year and look at what might happen to him in five years.

The Lowly Valued Employee

He makes $650 per week five years later but still produces $1,000 per week. His net value has decreased to $350 per week because his productivity remained stagnant. If his salary continues to increase at the same rate while his productivity stays the same, he'll be producing $1,000 a week and costing $1,000 a week in seven years. His net worth to the company will then be nothing.

The Run-of-the-Mill Employee

He makes $650 per week five years later and produces $1,250 per week. His productivity has increased by 25 percent but his net worth remains the same. His net value to the company hasn't increased in the five years he's worked there because his increase in productivity didn't outpace his salary creep.

The Highly Valued Employee

He makes $650 per week five years later and produces $2,000 per week. His salary has increased by over 60 percent but his net value has increased by 125 percent. His increase in productivity outpaced his salary creep. He has created the closest thing there is to true job security by making himself indispensable to his company. Companies would rather pay an employee $650 per week for $2,000 production than pay $400 per week for $1,000 production. This is a true win-win situation.

> Folks who never do any more than they get paid for, never get paid for any more than they do.
>
> Elbert Hubbard, 1856–1915,
> Author, Philosopher, and Publisher

Your Implied Warranty of Fitness

My great grandfather used to tell me about the good old days when a man's word was his bond. He said that business was done on a handshake and contracts weren't needed. He didn't know that a contract was created when men did business on a handshake. Three basic elements must exist in order to create a contract:

1. The first is an offer. This occurs when a company offers to provide a product to customers.
2. The second is acceptance of the offer. This occurs when a customer agrees to buy the product.
3. The third is consideration. This would include the price a customer agrees to pay as well as the terms of payment (net 30, COD, and so on).

Each party must also have the legal capacity to enter into a contract. For example, a 7-year-old couldn't create a legally enforceable contract. Someone of majority age has to sign on behalf of a minor. This is why a guardian must accompany a minor to a doctor's office.

Contracts don't have to be written as long as these conditions are met. Written contracts are the most easily enforceable, but there are other valid forms. An oral contract was created when my great grandfather shook hands with someone who agreed to do business with him. There are also implied contracts. These are the most ambiguous but can still be legally enforceable. Most people regularly enter into implied contracts without realizing it. Imagine that you go to dinner at your favorite steakhouse. A written contract isn't created because you don't sign anything prior to ordering the meal. An oral contract isn't created because you don't discuss payment arrangements prior to ordering the meal. The server brings you a menu. This is the restaurant's offer to feed you. Their prices are listed on the menu along with the forms of payment accepted (i.e., all major credit cards but no personal checks). This constitutes consideration. You accept their terms when you order from the menu. You have capacity because you're an adult of sound mind. An implied contract has been created. Next, the server brings you the bill for $40. You can't offer $20 to settle it. If you insist that $20 is all you'll pay, the restaurant can have you arrested for theft. They can't charge you with theft by taking because they freely served you the meal. They can charge you with theft by deception because you had an implied contract to pay the asking price. You have to honor the contract you created because you ate the entire meal.

The situation would be different if you bit into the steak and immediately realized it wasn't cooked to your satisfaction. The restaurant would try to cook it to your satisfaction or bring you another steak. They probably wouldn't require you to pay if they couldn't prepare it to your satisfaction, even though they'd have the legal right to do so. This is because of a commercial principle called *caveat emptor*, which means consumers are responsible for making certain what they buy is good quality unless the seller provides a guarantee. The short interpretation is "buyer beware." You might then defend yourself using a legal precedent called an *implied warranty of fitness*. A set of federal laws called the Uniform Commercial Code stipulates that implied warranties arise automatically when a product is sold. The law breaks implied warranties down into two categories: One is for fitness in general and the other is for fitness to a specific purpose.

A similar situation occurs when you accept a job offer. You create a written contract regarding your fitness for the job. You're offering to sell your service as an employee and the employer is accepting your offer based on the representations you made. We occasionally hear about people who get fired when employers discover they lied on their resume or job application. Individuals who lie to get a job are as dishonest as a car dealer who rolls back an odometer to sell a car. To fight this, employers often include verbiage on job applications such as:

> I understand that the company is relying on my truthfulness. I agree that if it should be discovered that the information I am providing is inaccurate, misleading, or incomplete in any respect, I will be disqualified for employment. If I have already been hired, my employment will be terminated immediately and I will forfeit all related benefits.

It's easy to catch people who lie on job applications. It's much harder to catch employees who cheat their employers in another way. You also create an implied contract of sorts when you accept a job offer. You're implying that you are willing to work hard and will give 100 percent. Your employer will still pay you 100 percent of your paycheck even if you only give 75 percent of your capabilities. Employees who do this are cheating their employer. They're also cheating themselves because their careers will suffer from mediocrity. You have an ethical obligation to earn every penny of your paycheck even though it may not be a legal obligation.

Conclusion

Highly valued employees earn every penny they're paid. This doesn't change no matter how long they've been with a company. Your company is making a big investment in you every day. Look closely at your next IRS W-2 form and ask yourself, "Was I *really* worth this much?" You're on your way to becoming a highly valued employee if you can honestly answer yes. If you can't honestly say you're worth every penny you were paid and have ethics, you have two choices. You can ask your employer to decrease your pay or you can increase your worth to your company. It's no more complicated than that. Both of you win when the latter is the case.

CHAPTER 6

Act Like You Own the Place

A good employee is one that will bend down and pick up a piece of trash in his path and not leave it for the janitor. He will answer the phone when it keeps ringing even though he is not he receptionist.

Karen McCarson, Program Manager,
Dimple Edward's Rehab, Longview, Texas

I've owned my own company since 1988. I often hear people say they'd like to own a business and I ask them why. Answers include:

"So I can set my own hours."

"To make what I'm really worth."

"So I won't have to answer to anyone."

I tell people who give answers like these to reconsider because they might be disappointed. They don't understand what owning a business really means.

Owning a business allows the freedom to come and go without permission from anyone, but it doesn't allow the freedom to come and go anytime the owner feels like it. Most business owners work more hours than their employees. The owner of a medical device manufacturing company in San Antonio recently told me that he can leave work any time he darn well pleases—after he puts in his 80 hours a week.

The desire to achieve financial independence is certainly a good reason to go into business. Tom Stanley and William Danko revealed that self-employed individuals are four times more likely to be millionaires than those who work for others in *The Millionaire Next Door*.[1] This has remained constant throughout history. George Eastman despised the poverty he grew up in during the nineteenth century. His father died when George was only eight and George swore he would ensure that his mother would be taken care of. He worked as a bookkeeper at the Rochester Savings Bank by day while experimenting with photography at night. He eventually founded Kodak and became one of the wealthiest men of his era. He would have never made his fortune working as an employee of the bank.

History is replete with stories of men like George Eastman who changed the way we live and became enormously wealthy in the process. Henry Ford and Walt Disney are two more examples. What many forget is that both Ford and Disney went bankrupt before they achieved such stunning success. For every Donald Trump, there are thousands of business owners taking cash advances off credit cards to make payroll. Some estimates have placed the average annual profit of small business owners in the United States to be as low as $10,000 a year. Owning a business greatly increases the owner's odds of becoming a millionaire. It also greatly increases the owner's odds of working for less than minimum wage. I caution people when they say that owning a business will help them make what they're really worth because they might not want to know how little that is.

Business owners don't have a supervisor to answer to. This doesn't mean they don't have people who hold them accountable. There are creditors who expect to be paid on time, customers who often demand the impossible, and sometimes a spouse who questions why they still can't pay the mortgage despite putting in 100 hours a week.

Hollywood has painted a highly unrealistic image of business owners. The mention of someone who owns a business conjures up images from greedy bank owner Mr. Potter in the 1946 movie *It's a Wonderful Life* to nuclear power plant owner Mr. Burns in the television show *The Simpsons*. Owning the company doesn't mean sitting in a leather wingback chair all day and counting piles of money while all the worker bees make more; it means quite the opposite. You'll never hear a business owner say, "That's not in my job description." Business owners refer to themselves as the chief cook and bottle washer because they have to do whatever needs to be done, whenever it needs to be done. This includes nights, weekends, holidays, and sometimes even birthdays.

Highly valued employees do whatever needs to be done, whenever it needs to be done.

A good employee comes to work every day and is always willing to stay over if necessary. Sound too perfect? I have one like that on my staff!

Rick Gersema, Cedar Falls Community Schools,
Cedar Falls, Iowa

No One Is Exempt

These truths aren't limited to owners of small businesses. They also apply to CEOs of big corporations. The annual income of the average CEO is higher than that of the average small business owner, but he or she still has to do whatever needs to be done. Look closely at the name tag of the flight attendant the next time you fly Southwest Airlines. It might read Herb Kelleher, Gary Kelly, or Colleen Barrett. They'll do their best to serve you but probably won't mention that this isn't their full-time position. Gary Kelly is the CEO of Southwest Airlines, Colleen Barrett is the president, and Herb Kelleher cofounded the company in 1967. Southwest encourages every employee to chip in and do whatever needs to be done. Pilots have helped load baggage, flight attendants have escorted customers through terminals, and mechanics have plowed snow. It comes as no surprise that they have defied the odds by remaining profitable while competitors filed for bankruptcy. Companies that wish to move from good to great, as Jim Collins put it, need employees who are better than good. They need highly valued employees who are indispensable to the company's mission.

CEOs also have to answer to boards of directors who can be very hard to please. Steve Jobs cofounded Apple Computer at age 20 with Steve Wozniak. He then served as CEO of the company until it grew to over 4,000 employees 10 years later. He was then fired at age 30 by his board of directors. A more recent example of how even the most high-powered CEO still has to answer to others is Carly Fiorina. She was one of the most powerful and widely respected women in business while serving as president and CEO of Hewlett-Packard from 1999 to 2005. Yet, all that power wasn't enough to save her when the board voted her out.

Even government officials must do whatever needs to be done and answer to others. Ron Serpas is the chief of the Metropolitan Nashville Police Department and manages over 1,200 police officers. He also drives a patrol car and hands out traffic citations just like any first-year officer would. He doesn't consider it beneath him because he's still a police officer, and police officers serve the public by keeping it safe.

Even those at the highest levels of government must also answer to others. The president of the United States is the leader of the free world. Yet a first-term president who doesn't please enough farmers in Iowa or retirees in Florida won't remain leader of the free world for another four years.

> There's only one boss—the customer. And he can fire everybody in the company from the chairman on down, simply by spending his money somewhere else.
>
> Sam Walton, founder of Wal-Mart

Employers have become accustomed to run-of-the-mill employees who only do what they have to in order to get by. This usually means what's printed in their job description and nothing more. Because of this, companies add "and all other duties as needed" as part of job descriptions. A highly valued employee doesn't need a job description to tell him what to do because he takes ownership. He does whatever needs doing without waiting until he's told what needs doing. He acts like he owns the place.

Why Staples Wants Its Employees to Act Like They Own the Place

Nancy Persson is vice president of organization development, training, and communications at Staples world headquarters in Framingham, Massachusetts. Staples is the world's largest seller of office products. It has over 1,600 stores, employs over 65,000 people, and reported over $14.4 billion in sales in 2004. Nancy told me Staples wants every employee (Staples calls them associates) to act like he or she owns the place. When I asked why, she responded, "Because people make good decisions when they act like they own the place." She explained that the industry has changed drastically since Tom Stemberg opened the first Staples in Boston's Brighton neighborhood in 1986. Staples' growth has been nothing short of phenomenal and made it a Wall Street darling. It reported a mind-blowing 20 percent earnings growth for 12 consecutive quarters from 2002 though 2004. Despite being an industry giant, Staples needs highly valued employees at all levels to continue its success. Convenient locations and good product selection have become common to them as well as to Office Depot and OfficeMax. To keep a competitive edge, Staples now seeks to make the difference with its people. Staples knows it can't get the level of customer service it wants unless every employee buys in to the company mission. It teaches its employees that everyone from cashier to CEO is personally accountable for results. Every employee is expected to act like he or she owns the place.

You Are an Extension of Your Company to the General Public

Walk into the offices of Courier Printing in Smyrna, Tennessee, and the first person you'll meet is Dottie Clancy. Dottie isn't the receptionist. The title on her business card reads "Director of First Impressions." I asked Dottie where she got this idea and she told me that Jeana Chicosky, the company president, takes her company's image very seriously. I typed "director of first impressions" into Google and found that the concept has become so big that there are now seminars on it. Apparently, many other companies also take it very seriously. These companies understand how critical every employee's role is to the customer.

Not everyone does. Many people underestimate their role in a company. No matter what an employee's position may be, he or she is the company's image to the general public. Customers don't know or care if an employee is a temporary worker or the company president. This is why companies need everyone to act like they are owners. Bad behavior or poor performance by one employee can permanently tarnish a company's image to a customer, and it doesn't have to be extreme for this to happen. One rude teller at a bank's smallest branch can result in a customer taking his or her business to another bank. To see how strongly customers identify entire companies with one employee, look at medical practices. Patients call and tell whoever answers the phone all about their maladies because they assume every employee knows how to treat them. They never realize the person they're talking to might be an 18-year-old receptionist with one week on the job. I used to joke about this with the receptionist at my veterinarian's office. I was fascinated with how many people called and expected her to remember Scruffy's symptoms from the last visit and know how to cure Scruffy's present ailment. I once heard her respond "I better let you speak to Dr. Alley about that" to four different callers in less than 20 minutes.

> I have 12 employees in production and 65 independent sales representatives. I teach them all that a consumer's attitude toward my company will be immediately formed as soon as they meet. What I can't do is undo a bad first impression. They *are* my company to my customers.
>
> Brian Frasier, President, Ergonomic
> Concepts, LLC, Clayton, North Carolina

The Customer Is Always Watching

Several years ago my company needed to purchase a highly specialized piece of equipment. I wasn't knowledgeable enough to make an informed decision and set out to learn as much as I could about the equipment. I visited each dealer in Nashville to determine which machine would best suit our needs. One dealer that carried such a machine is known for having the vast market share of a less complex line of equipment. My office manager discouraged me from visiting this particular company because she had encountered such poor service from them when she worked for a previous employer. She felt they were arrogant because they held such a large market share. I decided we shouldn't exclude a multibillion-dollar industry leader from consideration just because she had a bad experience with one employee years ago, and promised not to make a final decision before discussing it with her.

I visited the company and its sales manager pointed out a machine he recommended. I asked him to show me how it worked and he seemed surprised by my request. He then attempted to demonstrate but couldn't get it to work. He explained that he normally didn't have to demonstrate. I asked how he sold the machine to other companies without demonstrating it and he responded, "I normally just study applications, make recommendations, and take the order." I was appalled and wanted to walk out. I decided to stay and at least fulfill my mission of learning as much as I could. The sales manager next introduced me to their computer specialist who demonstrated software that would add several thousand dollars to the purchase price. As he demonstrated the software to me, he showed the sales manager a plane ticket he just received for a meeting in Knoxville. He had to fly from Nashville to Cincinnati to catch a connecting flight. This would take most of the day. I asked why he didn't drive since it only takes three hours to make the trip from Nashville to Knoxville by car. He explained that by flying he got to avoid working and spend more of the company's money. I was appalled again. It was bad enough that he held such contempt for his company that he wanted to waste their time and money. It was worse that he was discussing this in front of a customer. But it was unbelievable that the sales manager thought this was acceptable. He didn't act like he owned the company; he acted like he was at war with the company.

The biggest shock came after the demonstration. The sales manager still thought he had a sale despite everything that had happened.

He was truly surprised when he didn't get it. The equipment cost more than the car I was driving and I compared the experience to that of shopping for a car. Then I mentally apologized to all those who've ever sold cars for a living because the comparison was an insult to them. I've met many managers of car dealerships who exhibit the highest level of professionalism and demand the same from their sales department. The world's worst used car salesman wouldn't have been as unprofessional as what I experienced that day. A car salesman would have at least expected me to test drive a car before buying it and would know the sale was lost if the car wouldn't crank.

This incident happened 10 years ago and I suspect the two individuals have long since left the company. The company remains an industry leader but those two employees forged a company image that will linger with me forever. I've spent more on similar equipment since then than I spent on my first home, but never considered that one industry leader again. I shudder when I think of an employee actually getting a sense of accomplishment from hurting his employer.

> A good employee is a team player who feels a sense of ownership in the company.
>
> Diana Nester, Human Resources Manager,
> The Maiman Company, Springfield, Missouri

Conclusion

Regardless of what your position is, act like you own the place. This means you care about what happens to your company in the future as much as you care about what happens to yourself. The two are not mutually exclusive. By helping the company, you help yourself. By hurting the company, you hurt yourself.

CHAPTER 7

Treat Your Job Like It's Your Lifelong Career, Even If It's Only a Stepping Stone

I long to accomplish a great and noble task, but it is my chief duty to accomplish humble tasks as though they were great and noble.

Helen Keller

Think of all the workers you come into contact with as a consumer. How much they're paid or where they are on the corporate ladder is irrelevant to you. All you care about is how good they are at what they do and how professional they are in the way they go about it. You probably wouldn't return to a doctor who had a terrible bedside manner even if he saved your life. The attorney who never returned your calls and was disorganized when you spoke to her will probably lose you as a client even if she won your case.

I recently had the opposite experience at a Ruby Tuesday restaurant in Nashville. A young server named Annisha demonstrated exactly how a highly valued employee performs from the very beginning of the meal to the very end. It began when she brought out the meal. I hate it when I don't have enough sauce for my meal. I always order extra maple butter sauce with the Walnut Blondie at Applebee's, extra vanilla icing with Domino's CinnaStix, and extra barbecue sauce with McDonald's Chicken McNuggets. Servers at some restaurants sometimes forget my special request and put a real damper on the whole meal because the food is often cold by the time the server returns with the extra sauce. This wasn't the case with Annisha. I love Ruby Tuesday's Asian dumplings and always order extra Thai peanut sauce. I'm such a big fan of this appetizer that I often have it as an entrée. Annisha brought the extra sauce without prompting but she didn't yet know what a high-maintenance customer I am. I also love iced tea and it's next to impossible to keep my glass full. She was swamped with customers that night and I expected that I'd have to go easy on the spicy sauce since she probably wouldn't be back to refill my tea glass as often as I'd like. Somehow she managed to wait on all her other customers while refilling my glass four times. She then had the dessert menu ready just as I finished my entrée. The biggest test came next. My pet peeve is waiting for the server to bring the bill when I'm done eating and ready to go. Annisha had the bill ready just when I was ready for it. What made the whole experience so remarkable was what she did when she brought back my change. She looked me straight in the eye and said, "It's been a pleasure waiting on you and I'd like to wait on you again. Come back and see me." This was remarkable for two reasons. First, it had to be anything but a pleasure to wait on me. I kept the poor woman running the entire time. Second, something sounded odd about the way she said it. I've heard similar statements before but there was something different about Annisha's. I asked myself why I actually wanted to return and sit in her section again. Then it hit me. She had such sincerity and conviction that I actually believed her when she said it. The cynicism that we all develop as consumers temporarily faded away. The clerk at the department store who says, "How can I help you today" but has a look of boredom faded from memory. The cashier at the gas station who mumbles, "Have a nice day" but looks like he should be on "America's Most Wanted List" no longer tainted my perception of all service employees. I was fascinated at how my attitude changed. One employee's excellence at what she does actually became more important than the company's product. Ruby Tuesday has great food, but so do numerous other restaurants. They're in a similar situation as Staples competing with Office Depot and OfficeMax. What this particular restaurant had was a great employee who made the difference. This is why restaurant managers teach employees they're not just in the food and beverage business; they're in the hospitality business. People go to restaurants for more than food. They go for the experience.

> My daddy always told me that he would support me no matter what career decision I made. But if I was going to be a ditch digger, I better be the best ditch digger I can be.
>
> Rae Wagoner, Sun Publishing,
> Paducah, Kentucky

I Love My Job!

Go in to work tomorrow and proclaim out loud, "I love my job!" Then observe your coworkers' reactions. Those who are highly valued employees will likely respond, "Me, too!" The run-of-the-mill employees will quietly question your sanity. The lowly valued employees will try to infect you with their toxic energy by questioning your sanity out loud in front of others. They'll be appalled that you would be so outlandish as to actually make your job sound pleasant.

I recently observed what a positive impact a highly valued employee can have on morale at an Arby's restaurant in Clarksville, Tennessee. Michelle Reda is their manager. She was quietly humming when an employee asked if she was going to sing the song someone else sang. Michelle asked what song that was and the employee replied, "I love my job. I love my job. I love my job." Michelle responded, "I do love my job!" I asked why she loved her job. She said, "For one thing, I get to interact with great people." I thought perhaps she was new and this was a temporary optimism. I was wrong. Michelle is 34 years old and has been with Arby's for nearly three years. She was with a German restaurant for 10 years before that and with another fast-food chain before that. She's been in the restaurant business for 16 years and still maintains an amazing amount of enthusiasm and an incredibly positive attitude. I explained that I meet managers of every fast-food chain and many of them become quite cynical after so many years in such a tough business. I asked how she could remain so upbeat and sincere. She responded, "Your job is whatever you make of it." Her positive attitude has obviously served her well. Her employment history proves that her job is exactly what she chose to make of it. What began as a near-minimum wage job for an 18-year-old girl has turned into a rewarding career for an impressive woman. I know how highly Arby's values Michelle because her area supervisor happened to be in the restaurant that day. She noticed that I was talking to Michelle and taking notes. She thought I might be a headhunter and politely commented from the kitchen, "You better not be trying to recruit my manager!" Michelle's positive attitude makes her more than a highly valued employee and more than a manager. Seeing her employees' reaction to her positive attitude proves she is also a great leader.

> What makes a good employee? A general desire to want to do the best that you can!
>
> Pam Lewis, RN, Clinton County
> Outpatient Surgery, Wilmington, Ohio

How Important Is an Attitude?

I loved Norman Vincent Peale. I've read *The Power of Positive Thinking*[1] more times than I can count. I also admit that the Baby Boomer generation I belong to probably overhyped the concept of having a positive attitude in the 1980s. This contributed to the rebellious attitude toward corporate America led by Generation X and the grunge movement of the early 1990s. Corporate America has now come to some sort of middle ground in the new millennium. While most companies don't hold pep rallies and chant the company slogan, they still place an extremely high priority on their employees having a positive attitude. How highly do companies value employees' attitudes today? Just ask Todd Cassetty. He's a managing partner of Outback Steakhouse in Hermitage, Tennessee. When I interviewed him, I asked him to tell me about an outstanding employee. He immediately told me about a server named Denise whom he described as phenomenal. I asked what made her service so phenomenal and he explained that it wasn't her service that made her so special. Her service was phenomenal but what made her so special was her attitude. Denise would respond when asked how she was doing with, "Better than when I started my shift!" or "Great tips tonight!" Todd said, "She had no quirks and that made my job so easy." I asked Todd if I could meet Denise but he couldn't help me. Six years had passed since she worked for him at Outback's restaurant in Johnson City, Tennessee. She made such a lasting impression with her attitude that it still lingers with her former boss six years and hundreds of employees later.

The best example of how important attitude is comes from a company whose employees are more enthusiastic than any I've ever done business with. This company's employees are so committed to their mission that they're actually specified as my preferred provider when I travel. The company is Southwest Airlines, and their employees do for flying what Ruby Tuesday's employee did for my meal. They make it such an enjoyable experience that I want to come back just because of their employees. Every employee of every company who wants to secure a bright future needs to take a trip on Southwest Airlines just to observe their flight attendants, gate attendants, and pilots. Their commitment is the stuff of legends. I contacted their president, Colleen C. Barrett, to find out how they found so many highly valued employees. The following is an excerpt of the answers she gave.

Question: What do you look for in an ideal employee?
Answer: Our hiring process focuses on finding altruistic individuals who have a can-do attitude, a strong work ethic, and who are teamwork oriented. We often say we hire for attitude and train for skill, and that is

exactly what we do. We can't change a bad attitude, but we can train you to do just about anything we need you to do. Now, before you get nervous, we won't hire a pilot without flying experience, but we would turn down a pilot with proven excellent flying skills who displays a poor attitude.

Question: How is it that your employees are so pleasant? Are they trained to be that way?

Answer: We spend an inordinate amount of time and resources on the front end of the recruiting and hiring effort to be sure we find just the right person to come to work at Southwest. We use a process called targeted selection and peer interviews to help us find people who have just the right kind of Southwest Spirit and attitude. It isn't at all unusual for us to interview up to 100 people to find the right person for one job here at Southwest.

But What If You Hate Your Job?

Country music superstar Tim McGraw saturated the radio airwaves with his hit single "Live like You Were Dying" in 2004. Highly valued employees apply a similar philosophy to work. Treat your present job as if you plan on doing it for the rest of your life and you'll soon have a better job. You'll never get good enough at your present job to advance to a better one if you act as if your present job is beneath you. Jimmy Stewart wanted to get away from the small-town family savings and loan and take on the world in *It's a Wonderful Life*. He eventually realized that his present job offered everything he was looking for. He just needed to look a little closer. Michael J. Fox wanted to be a plastic surgeon in Beverly Hills in the 1991 movie *Doc Hollywood*. He got stranded in a tiny town in South Carolina on his way to California and was forced to work as a family doctor. After he matured and developed a better value system, he realized he loved the job in South Carolina. He also realized he would have hated the job in Beverly Hills.

It may not be possible to get excited about doing a boring job, but it is possible to give yourself a reason to look forward to going to work. If you have a job that really isn't that interesting and want to become a highly valued employee, find a reason to get yourself motivated about going to work. There's more to enjoy about work than the tasks we're paid to do. The people we work with, the environment we work in, and the customers we deal with can be rewarding if we let them.

But what if you've looked at these and still can't find anything to look forward to? Then create something. A dental hygienist in Oklahoma was struggling with this. She was so desperate that she had to take baby steps and keep reminding herself, "One day at a time. Just try to make it for one more day." The results were phenomenal. Mondays began with an office meeting that everyone dreaded. She decided she would open each meeting with a joke of the week. She had to work hard to develop this skill since she was terrible at telling jokes and hated public speaking. Eventually, she got good at it and other employees actually looked forward to her jokes. Tuesday was the day the uniform company delivered clean uniforms. The driver looked like Brad Pitt, so she called Tuesdays "the day Brad Pitt comes to see me." She had to get a little more creative about Wednesdays. She was on a diet and allowed herself one guilty pleasure each week, so Wednesdays became "hot Krispy Kreme doughnut day." The rest of the week was easy. Thursday was payday and Friday was Friday.

Let's look at how much difference her efforts made. The Monday morning joke got people to laugh. This put the people around her in better spirits which put her in better spirits. She went from complaining that her coworkers were miserable to be around to taking the initiative to do something that made them more pleasant. How she did it or what she did isn't important. The important part is that she was proactive enough to do something. She took action and the results were far more than expected. She only wanted to make work tolerable but ended up actually making it fun.

Skills, knowledge, professionalism, and communication are extremely important but they can be learned, developed, and strengthened over time. However, an outstanding attitude is a rare treasure. Simple but true, attitude is everything!

Jeannie Boudreau, National City Mortgage,
West Springfield, Massachusetts

Is it ridiculous that someone has to go to this extreme to find reasons to enjoy coming to work? No it's not. Many people work quite hard at finding reasons to be miserable. All of us know someone who has a good life but still finds something to whine about. The dental hygienist admitted that she was partially to blame for being so unhappy in the past because she had focused on the negative parts of her job. She only needed to shift her focus from the half of the glass that was empty to the half that was full. Now let's apply this to your present position. Write three things you like about your job in the following blanks.

1. _____

2. _____

3. _____

If you can't name three, name two. If you can't name two, name one. If you can't name one, resign immediately. You can't be passionate about your job if you can't name one thing you like about it, and you can't be good at it if you can't be passionate. You're not doing anybody any favors by staying at a job you can't be good at doing. Your boss may be a poor manager who's too weak to fire you and is secretly hoping you'll resign. You're also doing yourself and your family a great disservice by remaining in a position where you can't possibly excel.

A gentleman sitting beside me on a flight to Las Vegas explained his career dilemma. He was a maintenance technician at a printing plant in Alabama who told me he hated where he worked. He said he only stayed because there were no other jobs. I said, "Really? No other jobs whatsoever?" He assured me there were no local jobs in his field that would pay him what he was making and that he would have to drive 50 miles to another job that would be suitable. I explained that there were three things he apparently liked about his job:

1. It was local.

2. It paid well enough.

3. It was in a field he apparently wished to stay in.

His problem wasn't the job. His problem was that he didn't appreciate what he had. He pondered my response for a few minutes and
then went back to reading his book. He tapped me on the shoulder
as we were leaving the plane three hours later and said, "I've been
thinking about what you said. I do kind of like what I do. Maybe I
just needed a little reminder. Thanks."

> There's joy in work. There's no happiness except in the realization
> that we have accomplished something.
>
> Henry Ford

Being Passionate about What You Do Is a Choice, Not a Result

Can you still be passionate about your job if it isn't in the exact field
you'd like and doesn't pay as much as you'd like? You bet you can.
Just ask Janice Spencer of Milledgeville, Georgia. She's a custodian
at Georgia College and State University where I speak twice a year.
She comes to work at 6:30 A.M. every morning and is the only person in the building when I arrive around 7:00 A.M. She and I have a
routine every time I see her. She asks how I've been doing since she
last saw me. I always answer, "Better than I deserve! How have you
been Janice?" She always answers, "I am blessed." I have no doubt
she is blessed because her smile is so illuminating that I took a picture of it and put it on my web page. I'm also sure Janice is like this
at home because I met her daughter Juanitrice on my last visit. People call her Sunshine because she's so cheerful. I asked her how she
learned to be such a pleasant young lady and she responded, "That's
how my mamma raised me."

I also know there are some who might not think Janice is so
blessed. She's a single mom supporting five children on a custodian's salary. Yet, you would think Janice was doing brain surgery if
you saw her work. She takes such pride in what she does and is so
meticulous about it that her passion is inspiring. Another university
employee told me on my last visit how much Janice looks forward to
seeing me every six months. I made a point to let Janice know how

much I look forward to seeing her, too. That 30-second interaction we have twice a year inspires me to be better at what I do every time I walk into that lecture room.

> Every calling is great when greatly pursued.
>
> Oliver Wendell Holmes

Conclusion

Employers look for the same thing customers do. Companies are looking for employees who take great pride in what they do and do it well. Being good at what you do is unrelated to the task you perform. You must be the best you can be at whatever you do in order to be a highly valued employee. You don't have to be fiercely intense about your work, but you do have to be passionate in the way you go about it.

CHAPTER 8

Become the Most Reliable Person in Your Company

How do you know if your employee is good? Knowing that while you're away, the work gets done.

Anita Falco, Bridgeport Housing Authority,
Bridgeport, Connecticut

Being passionate about what you do is irrelevant if you're not there to do it. Just showing up can sometimes be more important in the long run than how well you do the job. Pete Rose is a prime example. He's one of the greatest baseball players of all time and holds over 30 records including:

- The most times at bat
- The most singles
- The most doubles
- The most career hits
- The most career runs

He doesn't hold these records because he had the most athletic talent. He holds them because of another record he holds—he played in the most games. He showed up and did his job. He wasn't always a standout player. He was never a home-run king like Babe Ruth, Hank Aaron, or Mickey Mantle. He was named the league's most valuable player only once despite having played 24 consecutive seasons, but he was the most dependable. That one quality earned him a place in the hearts of millions of fans including people from former President Jimmy Carter to myself. It's tough not to respect a man who is that devoted to what he does. The ultimate proof of how much fans admire Rose for his work ethic came after he went to prison for tax evasion. He emerged just as popular as when he was in baseball.

Abraham Lincoln demonstrated how important keeping one's nose to the grindstone is in the political arena. He lost local, state, and congressional races throughout his life. His persistence was finally rewarded by voters when he won his first political race, which happened to be for president of the United States.

Showing up and doing it consistently is critical to any career. Absenteeism is expensive for all businesses. A 2002 survey by Harris Interactive[1] found that unscheduled absences cost the employers they surveyed $789 per employee per year. You must have good attendance to be a highly valued employee. There's no way around this basic requirement.

> Coming from both a social work environment and a legal background, I've found excellent attendance and the maturity to responsibly report when unable to come to work to be highly valued in all arenas alike.
>
> Susan Petersen, Litigation Paralegal,
> Rice, MacDonald, & Winters,
> Myrtle Beach, South Carolina

If You Can't Be on Time, Be Early

Job longevity and good attendance are two of three components of being reliable. The third is being on time. The financial analyst of a

Tennessee automobile manufacturing plant told me it costs his company $10,000 for every minute their production line is shut down. One employee at the end of a production line can shut down everyone else in upstream positions. This bottlenecking problem was portrayed in a much replayed *I Love Lucy* episode in which Lucy worked in a chocolate factory. One employee who arrives five minutes late for work at the automobile plant could cost them $50,000.

Tardiness can also be very expensive in small businesses, including those that pay near minimum wage. This is often seen in day care centers. States require ratios of employees to children. The center can be shut down if too many employees are running late on a morning when state officials pay a visit. Even worse, children's safety can be put at risk.

When I scheduled an interview with Tennessee Deputy Commissioner of Personnel Nat Johnson for research on this book, I promised to limit our meeting to 10 minutes. Each of the other interviews for this book was done by phone but I wanted to meet Nat in person since we're both in Nashville. Our meeting was scheduled at 10:00 A.M. and I arrived at 9:45. The receptionist showed me to the conference room and explained that Nat was on a tight schedule but would be with me shortly. The first thing he mentioned when he walked in was how much he appreciated that I was early. Nat is a very busy man. The State of Tennessee employees over 44,000 people not counting higher education. He doesn't have enough hours in the day to waste a single minute waiting on people. He told me his philosophy is, "If you can't be on time, be early." He was so appreciative of my respect for his schedule that our 10-minute meeting went over a half hour. That one meeting also resulted in me signing on to help train every manager the State of Tennessee employs. I wouldn't have been invited to do this if I had showed up for our meeting late.

I applied the figures from the automobile plant to Tennessee's state employees just to see how expensive tardiness could be. If tardiness cost the state $10,000 a minute, Tennessee would lose well over $6 billion if every employee came to work 15 minutes late. Our state taxpayer's budget is less than $10 billion. This means the cost of absenteeism could exceed the state's entire budget if every employee was just a half hour late. This is a hypothetical example but illustrates how expensive tardiness can be.

You don't have to manage an organization with thousands of employees to appreciate the frustration of people showing up late. Just listen to how many laughs Jay Leno and David Letterman get at the expense of the cable television installer who keeps you waiting for hours. Or ask anyone who ever built a house what the most frustrating part of the process was. They won't tell you it was cost overruns, logistical problems, or agreeing on designs. They'll tell you it was the countless hours of waiting for contractors to show up.

Tardiness will cripple your career even if it doesn't cost your company a dime. It will make you very unpopular with your coworkers as well as your boss. Regularly dragging in to work late implies to the other employees that you don't have to be held to the same standard they do. Resentment always occurs any time one person isn't held to the same standards as others. I experienced this once while visiting family in Washington, DC. Parking is such a nightmare that good parking spots are the most highly coveted real estate in town. We were walking out of the Smithsonian Institute when I noticed a limousine parked in a no parking zone. I asked why this was allowed and learned that the limo belonged to a diplomat. They don't have to recognize U.S. laws because they have diplomatic immunity. They collect the parking tickets and throw them away. The same thing happens with diplomats at the United Nations in New York City. Foreign diplomats and consulates in New York received 143,508 tickets totaling more than $5 million in fines in 1996. Not one penny was paid. It comes as no surprise that local residents resent it and the resentment often turns into outright hostility.

Other employees have to cover for you when you don't show up on time. This will make you even more unpopular. You're showing disrespect for them by expecting them to do your job for you. Perpetual tardiness isn't the problem; it's the symptom. The problem is disrespect for the company, managers, and coworkers.

As a 47-year-old vice president and manager of an 83-year-old small family business, I've made a list of four fundamentals that every employee should have. I believe that no one who has these four fundamentals would ever be unemployed for very long:

1) Honesty.

2) Dependability. On time each and every day.

3) Basic math competence (addition, subtraction, multiplication, division).

4) Basic English competence.

Add a little politeness in with this mix and you have an employee that most, if not all, employers would jump at hiring and retaining.

Bill Buck, Buck Ice and Coal Company,
Columbus, Georgia

How Sticking to It Launched a Career with Lanier

I met Robert R. Young Jr. when he attended my management seminar in Augusta, Georgia. He was only 28 and had already been promoted three times in less than five years with Lanier. His inspiration for people who want to be highly valued employees isn't only in what he did after he was hired, but also in what he did to get hired. He went through Lanier's extensive interview process immediately after graduating college. The first stage is an informal meeting with a district manager. The second involves taking a Wonderlic test to evaluate skills and going on a one-day ride along with a sales representative. The third stage involves an in-depth interview with management. The fourth stage is when the final discussions are held and a formal offer is made. Robert made it all the way through the first three stages and then lost the position to another individual with sales experience. So did he get mad after losing the job he wanted so much? Absolutely not. He asked the district manager what he could do to make himself a better hire for the next company. The district manager told him to get sales experience and that's just what he did. Robert took a job selling cars on 100 percent commission with no base pay or draw against future commissions. He continued to call the district manager at Lanier once a month to update him on how he was doing and remind him that he would be coming to work for Lanier one day. After a year of selling cars, he was courted by a headhunter in Atlanta. He called Lanier back and told them he'd really rather work for them. It just so happened that a position had just come open and Robert walked right into the job he interviewed for a year earlier. He was hired as a commercial sales representative, promoted to senior sales representative one year later, promoted to account executive six months later, and promoted to sales manager one year after that. Today, he oversees both Augusta and Savannah. I asked what made him so successful in sales, thinking perhaps he had better closing skills than others. He explained that he's average. "Average?" I asked. "Then how did you advance so far so fast?" He explained that because sales is all about numbers all he had to do was work harder than anyone else and he would ultimately succeed if he just stayed with it long enough. He calculated that if his closing percentage was half of what another rep's was, he could still sell more copy machines than the other rep by calling on three times as many prospects.

Conclusion

You need to earn a reputation for being reliable in order to become a highly valued employee. This means your boss can be confident that you'll be there tomorrow and the next day, and you'll be on time. It also means you must do this for the long run. Anyone can come to work and be on time for a month or two. It's doing it year after year that matters. It is absolutely ridiculous when the only thing that stands between being a highly valued employee and a lowly valued employee is setting an alarm clock 30 minutes earlier. People who insist they can't make it to work on time don't have a time management problem. They have a problem with their priorities and apparently don't place a high enough value on themselves to be all that they're capable of being.

CHAPTER 9

Learn the Right Way to Make Mistakes

In order to be a highly valued employee, it's not necessary to be the best at your job. It is necessary to be the best you can be and do your job to the best of your capabilities.

Nat E. Johnson, Deputy Commissioner,
Tennessee Department of Personnel

Some people waste their lives trying to avoid making mistakes. This can cripple a career since perfection isn't attainable. They ultimately make fewer mistakes but accomplish less because they waste so much time trying to avoid making mistakes. Time is money in business. Doing a good job today is more profitable than doing a great job tomorrow.

Rock star Jon Bon Jovi's career might have ended before it started had he not understood this principle. He was only 21 when he won a contest with a radio station to record his first song in 1983. He quickly formed a band and released a debut album that went gold the following year. Suddenly, they were opening concerts for big names such as ZZ Top. They were rushed to record a second album and strike while the iron was hot. It was released in 1985 to poor reviews. Jon was unhappy with the album and had wanted to recut some of the tracks, but timing was critical. The band moved past this bump in the road and released their third album in 1986, but Jon wasn't completely happy with it either. He didn't think one particular song was good enough to be included on the album. Fortunately for him, his band, and his fans, he listened to the people who knew the business side of music. That song was "You Give Love a Bad Name." It became one of the band's best-known singles and helped send the album straight to number one on the Billboard charts. This launched them into super stardom and they went on to sell more than 100 million albums. They might have lost the support of their record label before they got to the third album if they had waited until the second album was perfect.

This is what happened to rock legend Tom Scholz. He's often referred to as the smartest man in the history of rock and roll. He holds a master's degree in mechanical engineering from MIT and is listed as an inventor on 34 U.S. patents. The 1976 debut album by his band Boston sold over 16 million copies and remains the biggest selling debut album in history. It's also considered one of the best-produced albums in rock history. Scholz played every instrument on every song and produced the album himself. He's brilliant and talented. He's also a consummate perfectionist who took eight years to finish the third album. CBS/Epic Records got tired of waiting, sued for breach of contract, and dropped Boston from their label.

Being a hair stylist isn't about always doing the best job. It's about consistently doing a good job so that the client never walks out unhappy.

Robyn Flynn, The No Name Salon,
Centerville, Ohio

Don't Confuse Having High Standards with Perfectionism

It's okay to have high standards as long as they're realistic. It's not okay to procrastinate until everything is exactly the way you want it to be. Your employer doesn't have time to wait until you get things perfect even if you are a genius inventor or legendary rock star. Deadlines must be kept and payroll must be met. An electrical engineer told me that he has to constantly remind the other engineers he supervises that sometimes 90 percent is good enough.

Perfectionist's careers suffer from their tunnel vision. They hyperfocus on minor details that often don't matter in the bigger scheme of things. Take the following steps to avoid this:

- Always look at the big picture instead of hyperfocusing.
- Accept the fact that you will make mistakes.
- Lower your standards to something reasonable.

Highly valued employees don't necessarily make fewer mistakes than run-of-the-mill employees or lowly valued employees. Highly valued employees often make more mistakes than their counterparts because the number of mistakes increases as productivity increases.

Imagine that you need to have your appendix removed. Two surgeons are available to do the procedure and you can select either. Two malpractice lawsuits have been filed against Dr. Smith for mistakes made during appendectomies. Both were settled out of court for undisclosed sums. No lawsuits have ever been filed against Dr. Jones. Which would you choose? You would probably choose Dr. Jones based on this limited information. The problem is that you can't make an informed decision because you don't have all the facts.

Imagine that you did some research that revealed that Dr. Smith has 30 years experience and has performed over 4,000 appendectomies. Dr. Jones has performed only three appendectomies since he's been in practice. Which surgeon would you now choose? Doctors know all too well that malpractice lawsuits don't always mean the doctor did anything wrong. Dr. Smith may have made no mistakes in either procedure but settled out of court because it was less expensive than going to trial. He would have over a 99.9 percent success rate even if he did make mistakes in two out of 4,000 procedures. This would be a phenomenal success rate in any profession including medicine. A 2003 study of rulings by medical examiners and coroners[1] found that the presumed cause of death was completely wrong 28 percent of the time. Few people who've been at their jobs for 30 years can say they have a 99.9 percent success rate. The attorneys who sued Dr. Smith probably don't have a success rate that high. Dr. Smith didn't make more mistakes than Dr. Jones because he's a less skilled surgeon. It was because he's a more experienced surgeon.

> The greatest mistake we make is living in constant fear that we will make one.
>
> John C. Maxwell

When Is It Okay to Make Mistakes?

Highly valued employees know the proper way to make mistakes. Making mistakes is okay under these conditions:

- They are reasonable mistakes to make.
- You catch your own mistakes.
- You correct your own mistakes.
- You accept responsibility and don't try to blame others.
- You don't make excuses.
- You don't hide your mistakes from your boss.
- You learn from your mistakes.
- You don't repeat the same mistakes.
- You apologize when it's appropriate.

Mistakes also get bigger the higher people climb up the company ladder. IBM founder Tom Watson once had an employee whose mistake cost him $600,000. Tom was asked if he was going to fire the employee. He replied, "No, I just spent $600,000 training him. Why would I want somebody else to hire his experience?"

Conclusion

Constantly making careless mistakes isn't acceptable but occasionally making reasonable mistakes is. The only way to avoid making a mistake is to do nothing. This is the most unacceptable mistake anyone can make since companies don't pay employees to do nothing. Making mistakes shows that you're doing something. Don't waste your resources on trying to avoid mistakes altogether. Instead, focus on how to minimize unnecessary mistakes and how to handle reasonable mistakes when you do make them.

CHAPTER 10

Broaden Your Circle of Influence

The most powerful people on earth are those who influence the most other people.

Jim Ziegler, Ziegler Dynamics,
Atlanta, Georgia

I was a joiner in my twenties. I belonged to Toastmasters International, chambers of commerce, civic organizations, alumni associations, and numerous other groups. It was the big 1980s and networking was the buzzword. I didn't join these groups to make society a better place; I joined to further my career. It was all about me. Looking back, I can admit that I was a self-serving narcissist. I'm now in my forties and am a huge Rick Warren fan who realizes the purpose of my life should be to serve others instead of serving myself.

Hindsight has also allowed me to see that my career probably suffered because of my shortsighted thinking earlier in my career. I withdrew from these organizations once my career began to take off when I was in my early thirties. Each was a fine organization that served noble purposes but no longer served mine. I made the mistake of distancing myself further and further from people who didn't have an immediate purpose in my daily affairs. This was a mistake for three reasons. First, I should have tried to help others who could benefit from my experience.

Second, I could have benefited from their personal support even if they couldn't provide professional support. One problem with distancing yourself too much from others is that it gets lonelier the higher you go in your career. There are few people to turn to when you're at the top. President Bush sought advice from Gerald Ford, Jimmy Carter, George H. W. Bush, and Bill Clinton. He didn't do this because he shared values and beliefs with all four of these men. Two were Democrats—members of the opposing party. He sought their advice because they were the only four living people who had held his job. This is why Bill Clinton sought advice from Ronald Reagan after being elected president. Being president of the United States is the most stressful job in the world. Just look at how fast both Bill Clinton and George W. Bush's hair turned gray once they became president of the United States.

The third reason it was a mistake to distance myself too far from others once my career began to take flight is that I was wrong in assuming that I no longer needed their professional support. I wrongly believed that successful people rely on others less than unsuccessful people do. The opposite is actually true. The U.S. Bureau of Labor Statistics reports that fewer than 20 percent of working Americans found jobs through networking, but a whopping 72 percent of the executives making over $100,000 a year did.

This was driven home for me in dramatic fashion in July 2005. I finally attended two meetings where I wasn't the speaker. This was the first time I had done this in years. Both were in Atlanta and I seriously considered backing out the weekend before I was scheduled to leave. I had just returned home to Nashville from a speaking engagement in St. Louis, was up against a deadline to complete the manuscript for this book, and would have to pack for four speaking engagements in Iowa the Sunday I returned from Atlanta. I decided to go to the meetings for two reasons that had nothing to do with the meetings. One was that I graduated from Georgia Tech's College of Management in 1985 and saw the trip as an excuse to take a trip down memory lane. I wanted to see my old fraternity house and have a chili dog at The Varsity, which is where I ate every week of my four years in college. My first two paperbacks were also about to be released and I saw this as a kind of triumphant return of the kid who barely graduated with a 2.3 grade point average. The other reason was that my executive editor was flying down from New York to attend one of the meetings. This provided an opportunity to spend some time with him, especially since we had done three books together and had never met in person.

The first meeting I attended was called the "Million Dollar Author Program," produced by Steve and Bill Harrison of Bradley Communications in Philadelphia. I was skeptical and a little turned off by the $3,000 cost to attend. It promised to teach up and coming authors all about getting publicity and how to make a book a best seller, but I was cynical. Since I was on my third book with a major New York publisher and knew virtually nothing about publicity and book promotion, I knew I needed to start somewhere. I figured Bradley was as safe a bet as any since they had worked with big names such as Jack Canfield and Mark Victor Hansen who wrote *Chicken Soup for the Soul,*[1] Deepak Chopra, and Dan Kennedy.

I begrudgingly drove to Atlanta with the preconceived notion that I wouldn't learn anything. The first night I attended a welcoming cocktail party. I introduced myself to Steve and asked him to point out my editor when he arrived. I then began to mingle and immediately met some of the wannabes. They were looking for a publisher and I was already signed. They wrote fiction and I write business books. Several of them wrote for fun and had no jobs. I write because it's part of my job. Apparently some of them were independently wealthy or married to spouses who supported them; I was neither. I started to wonder if I had wasted $3,000 and a precious week of my time. Then I remembered there was a money-back guarantee. Right as I was thinking about getting a refund and driving back to Nashville that night, Steve walked over and said, "Your editor just walked in the door." Darn! Now I had to stay. I had concluded my editor wasn't going to make it but it turned out his flight was just delayed. We talked business for a while and then called it an early night. The next day was "Meet the Agents Day" and it seemed like a waste of time. I didn't need an agent and again wondered what I was doing there. I made myself meet as many people as I could with the intent of learning something from each. I waited impatiently in a line to meet an acquisitions editor from Simon and Schuster, just in case I decided to try and become the next JK Rowling or John Grisham. I was about to give up and go to lunch when I noticed something familiar out of the corner of my eye. The woman in front of me was carrying a three-ring binder with a print out of her book's rankings on Amazon.com inside the clear overlay on the cover. She had hit number five. This is a feat that few authors ever achieve. Approximately 1,750,000 manuscripts are submitted to agents each year and only about 175,000 get published. Only one-third of 1 percent of those ever make any best-seller list. In the time it would have taken Harry Potter to twinkle his wand on this little muggle, I realized I was in the right place.

I introduced myself and heard the most amazing story. Her name was Sandy Forster and her best seller was titled *How to Be Wildly Wealthy Fast.*[2] She also hit number thirteen on *Business-Week's* best-seller list and didn't even know about it until she received an e-mail from a bookstore asking where they could find her book. What made her story so unique was that she lives in Australia and didn't have an agent, publisher, or American distributor. She self-published the book and wasn't even in Barnes and Noble. I shared her story with one of the literary agents at the meeting and he swore it wasn't possible to get on *BusinessWeek's* best-seller list without being in Barnes and Noble. Yet, there it was just as clear as day. I had lunch with Sandy and she introduced me to Peggy McColl from Canada. Peggy immediately earned my respect and admiration because she has written three books, *The 8 Proven Secrets to Smart Success,*[3] *On Being the Creator of Your Own Destiny,*[4] and *On Being a Dog with a Bone.*[5] I then learned that Peggy and her partner Randy Gilbert were the promoters who helped push Sandy's book to the best-seller list on Amazon and *BusinessWeek.* I became Peggy and Randy's newest client soon thereafter.

Next, I met Mahesh Grossman from California. He's a ghost-writing guru who earned my immediate admiration after I learned that he has been involved in the development of 45 books. He then flattered me by asking to include my story in his next book. What an incredible honor that was. Soon I found myself in an impromptu strategic planning session with T. J. Marrs from Oregon and John Long from North Carolina. In no time at all, they had helped me reposition my "Weekend Boot Camp for Managers" in Nashville to the "Glenn Shepard Executive Leadership Summit" in Las Vegas. I truly thought I had died and gone to heaven. These people were the chicken soup my soul badly needed for a long time.

The event's speakers over the next two days were phenomenal and my jaw never came off the ground. It all culminated with a four-hour presentation by Dan Kennedy who spent nine years on the Peter Lowe Success tour with Zig Ziglar and several former U.S. presidents. I met New York literary agent John Willig of Literary Services, Inc., who told me to look up a client of his named Lynn Robinson at the second meeting I was attending that week. Book marketing expert John Kremer from Iowa completely inspired me with the story of John Gray who wrote *Men Are from Mars, Women Are from Venus*.[6] His next book, *What Your Mother Couldn't Tell You and Your Father Didn't Know*,[7] hit the best-seller lists but paled in comparison to his previous book. So Gray returned to his first title and launched an entire series of *Men Are from Mars, Women Are from Venus* books and went on to become a publishing phenomenon.

I would have never met a best-selling author from Australia, promoter from Canada, ghostwriter from California, agent from New York, consultant from Iowa, or realtors from Oregon and North Carolina had I not taken time to attend that one meeting in Atlanta. So was this just a bunch of egomaniacs schmoozing and placating each other's egos? Absolutely not. The information gained and relationships created during that three-day conference yielded documentable results for me the very next week. It also produced big results for one individual before he even left the meeting. I introduced two attendees I thought could help each other and personally witnessed a $45,000 deal closed in about 15 minutes. This reminded me of an article I once read in the *Wall Street Journal*. It mentioned how many business deals are closed on golf courses and I suddenly understood why this is true. I was reminded that no man is an island unto himself. We all need the help of others no matter how successful we may be. The greatest irony was that the most successful and powerful individuals I met that week were the most generous and willing to help.

The business advice and support these people gave me was priceless. Just as priceless was the personal benefit. I was a completely different person when I left the meeting. I had a new attitude Patti LaBelle and Dr. Laura would have been proud of. Meeting others who shared some of my experiences felt like I was breathing fresh air for the first time in years. I imagine it is the way Tom Hanks' character must have felt when he was finally rescued from the deserted island in the 2000 movie *Castaway*.

The second conference I attended that week was the National Speakers Association annual convention. I had been a member for years but never attended a meeting. I didn't even make it into the Atlanta Hyatt Regency before the networking began again. I ran into Mike Stewart in the driveway. I had just met Mike at the other conference, where he taught me how to convert video files to run better on my web site and digitally record my seminars. We talked again and eventually I scheduled a return trip to Atlanta to spend three days in Mike's office. The technical training I got from him turned out to be a centerpiece of my company's new multimedia marketing strategy for seminars. I checked into the Hyatt and immediately called it a night. The next morning at breakfast I met Sheri Jeavons from Cleveland. She owns a training company and within minutes we both had pencils and notepads blazing. She wanted to increase her Internet sales so I referred her to Mike.

After breakfast, I set out to find the client the New York literary agent had told me to look up. I had no idea what she looked like and realized the exercise would be futile with 1,500 people attending the NSA convention. I was looking for a needle in a haystack. I crammed into the Hyatt's elevator to head to the first meeting and noticed the woman standing two feet in front of me was wearing a name tag that read "Lynn Robinson." She was the needle in the haystack I was looking to find. I almost expected the theme song to *The Twilight Zone* to start playing.

I was only able to stay at the NSA meeting for one day but learned just as much as I did at the previous meeting and made just as many connections. I now shudder to think about how many opportunities I might have missed over the years by becoming too isolated from my peers.

But what if you're not a public speaker or haven't written a book and don't have an agent, your own television show, or fan club? Do you still need to make connections with the people around you in order to succeed? You bet you do! You need the cooperation of other people to succeed no matter where you are in your career. The higher you go, the more you need to broaden your circle of influence. This is true for three reasons:

1. You can't become a highly valued employee unless you can get things done.
2. You'll need the cooperation of others to get things done.
3. You won't get the cooperation of others unless you have authority over them or influence with them.

You need to build your circle of influence and continuously broaden it. You don't have to schmooze to accomplish this. Simply be the kind of person people would invite to their house for dinner. I'm not implying that you need to go to your boss' or coworkers' homes for dinner in order to be influential. You should simply exhibit the same social graces that would make you welcome in their homes. This applies 100 percent of the time to 100 percent of the people you come into contact with on a daily basis.

> Even the brightest people won't make it with Marriott if they don't do well with people skills.
>
> Brendan Keegan, Executive Vice President of
> Human Resources, Marriott International,
> Washington, DC

The Difference between Friendship and Professional Relationships

Broadening your circle of influence at work doesn't mean building friendships; it means building working professional relationships. The difference between a friendship and a professional relationship usually lies in money. Both parties are in a true friendship only because they choose to be there. They enjoy each other's company, like each other, and share common values. Professional relationships are about business. One or both parties are usually paid to be there. You don't have to share values with people, enjoy their company, or even like them to have a working professional relationship. You probably couldn't tell me what your CPA's hobby is. You might not even personally like her. Yet, you would probably continue being her client if she's an extremely good accountant.

> The most important single ingredient in the formula of success is knowing how to get along with people.
>
> Theodore Roosevelt

Don't Rain on Other People's Parades

Highly valued employees know how to build healthy relationships. One key to doing this is not to rain on other people's parades. This principle applies in both personal and professional relationships. Imagine that you received a perfect score on your performance evaluation and earned a $1,200 raise. You want to celebrate by taking your spouse out to dinner. You get home and proudly announce your good news. Your spouse responds, "I've got some news that's not so good. The transmission is about to go out on my car." You're furious that your parade was rained on but aren't sure if you have the right to feel that way. There's no way both of you can make it to work if the transmission goes out. You commute 25 miles to work in one direction and your spouse commutes 25 miles in the other. You've both used all your paid time off for the year and one of you will have to take unpaid time off while the transmission is replaced. That's assuming you can even come up with the money. Your emergency fund is already depleted because your water heater went out last week. It seems as though Murphy's Law has become a metaphor for your life. These are dire circumstances and the situation must be dealt with soon. It didn't, however, have to be dealt with at the exact moment you were announcing your raise. The transmission problem would have been no worse if your spouse had held back the bad news just long enough to allow you to have your 15 minutes in the spotlight. You then explain how you planned on going out to celebrate your accomplishment at your favorite restaurant. Your spouse says "All right, let's go," but you no longer have the desire to do anything. Your moment of glory has passed. Your parade was rained on and you feel cheated.

You're off the next day and take the car to the shop. It turns out the transmission fluid was low and it cost less than $20 to solve the problem. You'll immediately go through a litany of emotions. You'll first feel relieved because a burden has been lifted off your shoulders. Then you'll feel elated as if you just won a prize. Then you'll realize you lost your moment in the spotlight over $20. You'll feel resentment that may even turn to anger. You worked hard all year to earn that $1,200 raise only to have your accomplishment upstaged by a $20 repair. To make matters worse, the feeling of being robbed will linger long after the pleasant memory of the dinner would have faded.

Now let's look at how different the outcome would have been if your spouse had held the bad news until a more appropriate time. Imagine that you announced your good news and the two of you went to dinner to celebrate. You'll eventually get tired of talking about your raise and ask how your spouse's day was. He or she tells you it wasn't so good but doesn't want to rain on your parade. You insist on hearing the news and suddenly the transmission problem isn't so bad. In fact, it's good timing. It no longer diminishes the significance of your raise. It now increases it because you saved the family from a potential financial crisis. You'll both benefit from your spouse's better timing because:

- You got to have your moment in the spotlight.
- Your raise just became a much bigger event.
- You demonstrated your unselfishness by using your raise to repair your spouse's car.
- Your spouse demonstrated his or her unselfishness by thinking of you before blurting out bad news.

The ability to deal with people is as purchasable a commodity as sugar and coffee, and I will pay more for that ability than any other under the sun.

John D. Rockefeller

The Importance of Showing Self-Restraint

Sigmund Freud described people who are obstinate, meticulous, or uptight as having an anal-retentive personality. Most people know this term and have used it to describe someone they've encountered in their lives. What most people don't know is the term that Dr. Freud used for people with the opposite characteristics. He described individuals who are disorganized, reckless, careless, and defiant as having an anal-expulsive personality. All humans are like this as infants. Infants don't care about where they are, the time of day or night, or if they're wearing a diaper. They give in to urges whenever and wherever they occur because they haven't yet learned the concepts of discipline or self-control.

Learning to control our urges until the appropriate place and time is part of growing up. Most of us learn to control our most basic biological urges somewhere around the second year of life. We develop a fully functional vocabulary a few years later. Most of us then learn when to speak and when to keep quiet. Hormones start to rage when we hit puberty. We then develop sexual urges that we must learn to control. Most of us have a fast enough metabolism that we can eat whatever we want without considering the consequences at this age. Next we start our careers and begin earning a respectable income in our twenties. Most of us then spend our twenties getting into debt and gaining weight and then spend our thirties trying to undo the damage.

Many adults lack the discipline to deal with issues until they're forced to deal with them. Eventually, people are forced to deal with their lack of discipline in eating when they become morbidly obese and develop heart disease or diabetes. People are forced to deal with their out-of-control spending habits when their car is repossessed, they're evicted from their homes, or file for bankruptcy. People are forced to deal with failure to control their sexual urges when they encounter an unplanned pregnancy or a deadly disease such as AIDS. The one thing many adults never learn to control is their mouths.

> Remember not only to say the right thing in the right place, but far more difficult still, to leave unsaid the wrong thing at the tempting moment.
>
> Benjamin Franklin

Have you ever noticed how a married couple will lie to each other while children speak the brutal truth? A man will lie to his wife when she asks if an outfit makes her look fat or if he notices the crow's feet around her eyes. A woman will lie to her husband when he asks if he makes enough money or still looks handsome since he lost most of his hair. We expect our spouses to be tactfully truthful but not brutally honest. Ask your kids any of these questions and they'll lay the unabashed truth on you. They don't consider the consequences of blurting out whatever they're thinking.

I recently experienced how beneficial it is in the workplace when people consider the timing of what they say before they say it. I had just received an e-mail from my executive editor informing me that the publishing committee had approved the proposal for my third book and a contract was on the way. This was a proud moment for me. I strolled through the office to announce the news. One of my employees was on the phone so I came back to her later. She smiled, congratulated me, and shared in my brief celebration. Later that day, I learned that the phone call she had been on was with her 22-year-old daughter who was calling to tell her mother that she had cancer. My heart dropped. My first concern was for my employee's daughter and her health. My second concern was for my employee and her anguish as a mother. I expressed my sympathy and then asked why she didn't mention the situation when I was bragging about my new book deal. She explained that she had seen how hard I worked on the previous two books and knew my moment in the sun would soon be eclipsed by grueling months of writing, research, and editing. We later learned that her daughter didn't have cancer. It had been a false alarm. Yet, that one incident when my employee thought about what was important to me before she spoke caused me to appreciate her even more than I did before.

This incident was personal and had nothing to do with business. Still, I appreciated the way she handled the situation so much that I know it will influence certain business decisions I make regarding her. Last year she earned a $4,000 year-end bonus. The phone call incident will still be in my mind when I consider her year-end bonus this year. I pay my employees well and know I could fill each of their positions for less money. My accountant has even suggested that I consider paying them less so that I can pay myself more. I choose to pay them well because I believe my employees are the best investment I can make. This particular employee confirmed that I have invested in the highest quality people at my company.

Learn to Let Others Have the Spotlight When It's Their Turn

Spouting out bad news is a sure way not to broaden your circle of influence. Another is to compete for the spotlight. Imagine that it's your birthday and your spouse throws you a surprise birthday party. This is the one day of the year that should be all about you and no one else. Your sister stands up in the middle of the party and announces that she just got engaged. You'll be happy for her but won't be happy about her stealing the spotlight from you. This day wasn't supposed to be about her. Her wedding day will be about her. She'll also have months to tell everyone about her engagement but you may never have another surprise birthday party.

Adults who always have to be the center of attention are selfish just as children are selfish. Adults who always have to be the center of attention are still behaving as children. They won't have influence with others and will never become highly valued employees.

> At UPS, it's all about the "we" and not about the "me."
>
> Lea Soupata, Senior Vice President,
> Human Resources, UPS

Make Whatever Is Important to the Other Person
Be Important to You

The first thing a sales representative learns is to immediately scan a prospect's office for what's important to him. The easiest thing to spot is a picture of a spouse and kids. Grandkids and pets are even better since people have less opportunity to brag about them. Hobbies are next. Any trophies also make an easy target.

Sometimes it isn't clear when people want us to acknowledge an event or what the event is. One classic example Dr. Laura uses is that of a woman who comes home and asks her husband if he notices anything different about her. He tries but doesn't notice that she changed her hairstyle. She may perceive him as being inattentive but he sees it differently. Hair just isn't that important to men, especially since we tend to lose it as we get older.

Most times it isn't this difficult to figure out what others want us to notice. We only need to listen. People will usually let you know when something is important to them by bragging about it, showing pictures, or making announcements. Celebrate events with others if it's important enough for them to share with you, no matter how trivial the event may seem to you. Celebrating our children's successes is how we nurture children's development; celebrating our peers' successes is how we nourish adult relationships.

Sometimes, it's not a matter of celebrating with people but merely showing interest in what interests them. This is easy if it's an interest you share. This becomes more challenging when their interests bore you or you just can't relate. Many years ago, I took a class in stand-up comedy to improve my skills as a public speaker. The instructor taught us the importance of commonality on the first night of class. He rubbed his eyes and said, "Doesn't it feel so good when you take your contact lenses out at night and can do this?" Those of us who wore contact lenses immediately identified with him. The rest of the audience didn't get it. He used this to demonstrate the importance of a stand-up comic choosing a subject matter that's common to the entire audience. He then used an example of how annoying it is when you're standing in the express line at the grocery store under a sign that reads "10 items or less" and the guy in front of you is unloading 200 items out of his cart. Everyone related and he got a thunderous round of applause.

Sometimes the subject the other person wants to talk about is common enough for you to relate to but is boring because it's from a past stage of your life. Teenage girls' conversations often revolve around who's dating whom. Teenage boys' conversations often revolve around who has the loudest car stereo. College age kids' conversations often revolve around who had the best party last night. In the late twenties, people's conversations often revolve around who's getting married or having a baby. Thirty-somethings' conversations often revolve around the latest award their kids won. Forty-somethings' conversations often revolve around where their kids are going to college. Fifty-somethings' conversations often revolve around plans for retirement. Sixty-somethings' conversations often revolve around their grandkids. Seventy-somethings' conversations often revolve around their health problems and eighty-somethings' conversations often revolve around who died. Does this sound familiar? You've probably held several of these conversations at some point in your life. Subjects that seemed like the most important thing in your life at the time are probably irrelevant to you now that you're at a different life stage. Regardless of your present life stage, you must show interest in what's important to others if you wish to build human relationships of any kind.

Celebrating other people's victories shows you care about them and that your world doesn't revolve around yourself. But what if someone really was the most self-centered narcissist in the world? You should still celebrate other people's victories even if your only concern is for your own well-being because you'll need others to also care about your well-being. You can't expect others to care about you if you boldly demonstrate that you don't care about them.

> You can have everything you want in life if you will just help enough other people get what they want.
>
> Zig Ziglar

Conclusion

You don't need to establish personal friendships with your coworkers but you do need to build strategic alliances. You'll need to know how to influence people and broaden your circle of influence in order to do this. People today have lost many of the social graces. You should tune yours up if you want to influence others. People notice you even when you don't realize it. People also have long memories and one little comment or misstep can hurt your career for years to come.

11

Adopt the Work Ethic Your Grandparents Had

A price has to be paid for success. Almost invariably those who have reached the summits worked harder and longer, studied and planned more assiduously, practiced more self-denial, overcame more difficulties than those of us who have not risen so far.

Barry C. Forbes

The American work ethic has been in a state of decline for the past two decades. One reason for this may be because we have attained such a high standard of living that people take it for granted. Most of us have easy lives compared to our grandparents. The U.S. Department of Labor reported in July 2003 that earnings averaged $16.98 per hour for private industry and $22.22 per hour for state and local government employees.[1] A 40-year low interest rate has made home ownership more accessible than ever. The Federal Housing Finance Board reported that the national average one-family house purchase price in November 2004 was over $264,000.[2] People appreciate what they have when things get tough, but it is easy to take things for granted when life is as good as it is today.

My great grandfather used to warn me to be scared of bad times because they're always just around the corner. I used to think he exaggerated because he lived through the Great Depression. I now appreciate the wisdom of his words 20 years after his death. People today are living far above their means and most don't realize it until they face a catastrophic event such as losing a job. It's important to keep our high standard of living in perspective. Failing to do so can lead to a false sense of accomplishment that can lead to complacency at work. Don't let past successes become an excuse to start coasting and ultimately lead to failure. Military commanders know that complacency in a time of war is a soldier's worst enemy. It's easy to keep your guard up when mortars and grenades are exploding all around you. Highly valued employees don't let past successes become an excuse to rest on their laurels.

> Something in human nature causes us to start slacking off at our moment of greatest accomplishment. As you become successful, you will need a great deal of self-discipline not to lose your sense of balance, humility, and commitment.
>
> Ross Perot

Another reason for the declining work ethic has been the drastic shift in attitudes about work. Our country respected hard work and success in the 1980s. This was largely a by-product of the value system of the Baby Boomer generation discussed in Chapter 4. There was a general upheaval against traditional values in the 1990s. This was led largely by the rebellious Generation X. Workaholic Baby Boomers who toiled to the point of neglecting their families in the 1980s went too far in the direction of work. Then the slacker grunge movement that largely denigrated career professionals in the 1990s went too far in the opposite direction. Hard work actually got a bad name because of this.

You must adopt a strong work ethic if you are to become a highly valued employee. Most rank and file employees tell me they have a strong work ethic. Most managers disagree. As Dr. Phil would say, you have to "get real" about your work ethic if you want to become a highly valued employee.

Death by Overwork

It is often said that hard work never hurt anyone. This isn't completely true. The Japanese face a problem called *Karoshi*. This is interpreted in English as "death by overwork." It was originally called "occupational sudden death" with the first reported case of a 29-year-old newspaper employee in 1969. Men were suddenly dropping dead without any sign of poor health but the problem wasn't officially recognized until the late 1980s. The Japanese Labor Ministry reported 21 cases of *Karoshi* in 1987, 29 cases in 1988, and 30 cases in 1999. Japan's National Liaison Council of Lawyers on Death from Overwork argues that as many as 10,000 cases of *Karoshi* occur each year. We may never know the exact number but we do know that Japanese men regularly work 12-hour days, 6 days a week. Some *Karoshi* victims were working more than 100 hours each week with no overtime pay. They were competing with coworkers who brought enormous peer pressure and worked themselves to death out of a samurai-like pride. Compare this to hourly workers in the United States who are guaranteed time and a half for working over 40 hours a week and it becomes clear that *Karoshi* isn't a problem here. I suggest to whiners who think that working a 50-hour week is murder that they move to Japan and try working a 100-hour week.

Don't Confuse Working Hard with Workaholism

Early in my career, I worked as an assistant plant manager at a production facility. I avoided walking through the breakroom when frontline employees were on break because I got tired of hearing them complain about not making enough money. Yet, few hands ever went up when I asked for volunteers to work Saturday at time and a half. Their paradigm wasn't to work more hours to increase their income. They only wanted the company to increase their wages for the hours they did work. Ironically, the employee who complained most about being underpaid was the one who averaged the fewest hours. She rarely put in 40 hours in any given week.

Some people mistakenly believe that hard work causes them to sacrifice quality of life. It doesn't. Constantly working obsessively to the point of seriously damaging relationships and other life pursuits does. This isn't the same as working hard. Work should not be the purpose of your life; it should only be a means to an end. For an 18-year-old, it might be to buy his first car. For a 24-year-old single mom, it might be to feed her kids. For a 30-year-old couple, it might be to buy a house. For a 50-year-old, it might be to take early retirement. Working hard is necessary to survive and it's the only way we can achieve most of life's biggest goals. Constantly working obsessively for no reason is workaholism. Working hard with a goal in mind is called focus. Having focus is healthy; workaholism is not. Highly valued employees don't suffer from workaholism but benefit from hard work.

Hard Work Can Keep You Young

Paul Harvey summed it up best when he said, "All things in moderation." Mr. Harvey worked hard his entire career and could easily have afforded to retire young. Instead, he signed a 10-year contract extension with ABC in 2000 at the age of 82. Those who didn't understand why a financially independent man in his eighties would continue getting out of bed at 3:30 every morning didn't understand Mr. Harvey's motivation. He admitted on numerous occasions that despite his steadfast loyalty to his loving wife Angel, he carried on a love affair with one other—the microphone. Work didn't make Mr. Harvey old before his time; it did quite the opposite.

Work can actually keep us young when we go about it the right way. Mr. Harvey wrote thank you letters to other networks who courted him when his contract was up for renewal in 2000. One wrote back, "We'll reopen talks in 10 years. I'll get you yet." Other great achievers such as Peter Drucker, Billy Graham, and Norman Vincent Peale worked into their eighties and nineties. George Burns was scheduled to perform in Las Vegas on his 100th birthday and came close to making it. Each of these men worked hard but were not workaholics. We can draw this conclusion because one price lifelong workaholics often pay is that of failed marriages. George Burns remained married to Gracie Allen for nearly 40 years until her death while these other super achievers remained married for over 60 years. These five great men proved three points:

1. Hard work is not inherently unhealthy.
2. Hard work doesn't decrease the quality of life.
3. Hard work can actually keep us young.

Don't Let Others Pull You Down

You may come to the conclusion that you haven't been working hard enough in your career to be a highly valued employee. If you decide to change this, do so with a warning. People have a strange habit of discouraging others anytime they try to improve themselves. This applies to everything from finances to health to careers.

I constantly encounter this when people discover that I've never personally bought a new car.[3] I've always known that a high-quality used car is a far better deal than a new one that loses 25 percent of its value the day it's driven home. My philosophy on this was confirmed in 1996 when Tom Stanley and William Danko reported in *The Millionaire Next Door*[4] that the average millionaire never buys new cars and later by financial guru Dave Ramsey. Yet, the people who mock me for this the most are those who are drowning in a sea of debt including huge car payments.

I also encountered this in 1999 when I went on a low carbohydrate diet. I was amazed at how quick people were to tell me the diet was unhealthy and that I should get off it immediately. Many were graphic in describing how all the red meat would block my arteries and kill me. None of those critics ever cared enough to learn that I actually ate more fish and chicken once I started the diet, and far less red meat than I ate before I started it. My cholesterol dropped dramatically and I lost 52 pounds, which I have kept off. I find it ironic that none of those critics ever said, "Glenn, you're fat and it's bad for your health. You need to lose weight" before I went on the diet. Their criticism only came once I tried to improve my situation.

The same will happen to you when you try to improve your work ethic. There will be people in your life who will discourage you from working harder. They'll purport to be concerned about your well-being but their concerns could be far less noble. If they were really concerned about you they would inquire about your financial situation or goals and offer you encouragement. Their real concern may be that they look lazy if you work too hard. They'll say things such as:

"There's more to life than work."

"Don't get so busy making a living that you forget to make a life."

"Don't forget to smell the flowers along the way."

Look closely and you'll notice most of them can't afford any flowers to smell.

This habit of pulling people down when they try to improve themselves isn't limited to humans. John C. Maxwell tells a story of a study done on how animals can pull each other down. Four monkeys were locked inside a room with a pole in the middle. A bunch of bananas hung from the top of the pole and one monkey tried to climb the pole to get them. The experimenters hit him with a blast of water that knocked him off the pole just as he reached the bananas. Each of the other three monkeys tried to reach the bananas and each was knocked off the pole by a blast of water. Eventually they all quit trying. The experimenters then replaced one monkey with a new one who didn't know about the water hose. He immediately tried to climb the pole but was pulled down by the others. The experimenters replaced each monkey one by one. Each new monkey tried to climb the pole and was pulled down. Eventually there were four monkeys who had never been hit with the blast of water. None of them would climb the pole but none knew why. Don't let the monkeys in your life pull you down while you're trying to climb the ladder of success.

Remove Self-Imposed Limits

The only way to measure something is to compare it to something similar. Homes are appraised in comparison to how similar houses in the neighborhood are selling. Your employer determines what wages must be paid by looking at what other employers are paying for similar positions in the market. The measuring stick you use in assessing your work ethic is going to greatly affect your self-evaluation. You'll feel like a slacker if you compare yourself to the Japanese who work 100 hours a week until they drop dead from *Karoshi*. You'll feel like a workaholic if you compare yourself to a 30-year-old who's still living with his parents and only working 20 hours a week because he's been attending junior college for the past 10 years.

One bias you should be careful to avoid is the Hawthorne Effect. This term came from a 1924 study General Electric (GE) commissioned at an Illinois light bulb plant. Researchers informed production workers they were going to increase lighting in the plant to determine if it would increase production. The lighting was increased and production also increased. Researchers then informed workers they were installing more lighting to see if production would increase again. Additional lighting was installed and again production increased. GE thought they'd be able to sell unlimited light bulbs to businesses by promising that additional lighting would increase productivity. Then one of the researchers popped the bubble of marketing nirvana by suggesting that productivity didn't increase because of the lighting, but because the workers knew they were being monitored. To prove this, the experimenters told workers lighting would be increased again but only pretended to do so. Production increased anyway. The researchers learned that productivity increases when it's monitored. They also learned that people have a preconceived notion of what their maximum capacity is, and this self-imposed limit is usually set arbitrarily.

This is the dilemma of personal growth. We don't grow unless our limits are pushed and most of us resist attempts by anyone who tries to push us further than we want to push ourselves. Sometimes it's events that force us to grow. Ask the parents of any large family how overwhelmed they felt when their first child was born. The amount of time and energy that one little creature demanded was overwhelming. Every waking minute was about him. Sleeping through the night was a luxury they thought they'd never see again. They had their moments of doubt when they wondered if they could do it. Then came their second child and having just one looked like a walk in the park. Suddenly there were twice as many diapers to change, twice as many visits to the pediatrician, and even less time for themselves than before. Then came the third child and having two seemed like a distant fantasy. The cycle continued as each child was born. They always saw themselves as functioning at maximum potential regardless of how many children they had. The birth of each additional child raised the bar to a new level they never knew they could reach.

This applies in all areas of our lives. I experienced this recently in my exercise regimen. I used to be an avid jogger but ran less and less as my travel schedule became busier over the years. Last year, I swore I would resume running on a regular basis. My goal wasn't distance, just consistency. At first it was to jog 30 minutes once every week. This was an easy goal I couldn't miss achieving. Then the old faithful jogging watch I'd used for years broke. It was a plain and rather unattractive one I bought on sale at Kmart years ago so I didn't mind shopping for a new one. I drove to Target and was amazed at how much jogging watches had changed since I last bought one. Rubber watchbands had been replaced by a woven material with Velcro fasteners. The displays were much larger and easier to read in bright sunlight. Intermittent timing made it easier to pace and they were all much more attractive than my old one. I picked out the most athletic looking model they had. I couldn't wait to get home and try it out. I strapped it on and went out for my first run as the proud new owner of an Ironman Triathlon watch. I played with all the buttons on my new toy as I ran by Nashville's Percy Priest Lake where I had jogged for years. I became more fascinated the more I played with it. I passed one marina and then another. I never noticed the sweltering summer heat. I had run for an hour by the time I returned home from my intended 30-minute jog. I only wanted to form a habit of consistently jogging 30 minutes each week, but I couldn't possibly stop at 30 minutes when I went jogging the next week. I had raised the bar without trying. One hour became my new standard. Soon once a week wasn't enough and before long I was running with thousands of other runners in public road races. It was only when I accidentally distracted myself that I no longer placed self-imposed limits on how far I went.

The last three or four reps is what makes the muscle grow. This area of pain divides the champion from someone else who is not a champion.

Arnold Schwarzenegger

Conclusion

You don't need to work yourself to death to become a highly valued employee. You also don't need to become a workaholic. You do need to create a strong work ethic. Instead of wasting time looking for shortcuts to success that don't exist, take the path less taken. That path is good old-fashioned hard work. Attitudes toward work have changed as different generations have come and gone and hard work got a bad reputation along the way. Regardless of your generation, hard work is a necessity if you're to become a highly valued employee. Push your limits and you'll be amazed at how much you can grow and thereby increase your value in the job market.

CHAPTER 12

Be a Professional at Whatever You Do

Some of the best employees I have ever had the privilege to work with were not the smartest or fastest, but they had a heart and attitude to do their best everyday. I would take one employee with heart and a positive attitude over ten faster or smarter mediocre people who were just collecting paychecks.

Pamela V. Adams, Vice President, Covenant
Mechanical Contractors, Atlanta, Georgia

I don't trust people to do what they say they're going to do until they actually do it. It's not that I'm so distrusting by nature; it's just the way trust works. People have to earn your trust; you can't give it to them. This is even truer when money is involved. There seems to be an epidemic of incompetence today and I feel like the most frustrated consumer in the world. I've tried cajoling, challenging, and begging people to do what they say they're going to do. I once set out to see how bad the incompetence problem really is by keeping a journal. The following is an excerpt:

Monday

We received the highly specialized voice-mail machine we spent two weeks trying to locate. The sales rep told us it had a 32-minute outgoing announcement capacity that we planned to use to record an audition of my seminar. Instead, it had an outgoing announcement capacity of 32 seconds.

Tuesday

The first e-mail quote came in from a radio announcer to narrate my new book on audio CD. He quoted the project at $100 but later explained that he meant $1,000.

Wednesday

The company that sold us the wrong voice-mail machine quoted us the correct machine for $300. It turned out to be $900.

Thursday

Three different employees of a major home improvement store told me that I could go into the granite fabrication shop and choose where the cuts would be made on my new kitchen countertop. When I arrived, I was told customers aren't allowed in the shop and I had to accept the cuts wherever they chose to make them.

Friday

The receptionist at the car dealership swore "on her mother's grave" that the only problem with my car was that it needed a routine 60,000-mile oil change and service that would cost $36. It needed the coils replaced and the repair cost $500.

Saturday

I received a letter from the governor's office of a certain western state telling me they had no budget to attend my seminar. Oddly, I never asked them to attend my seminar. I asked for a 10-minute phone interview with someone from the governor's office to discuss what they looked for in an ideal employee. I suppose it shouldn't have been a surprise that four words in the letter were misspelled.

Sunday

I called before leaving Nashville to confirm my hotel reservation that night near Cincinnati. The front desk clerk confirmed that I had a king size, nonsmoking room guaranteed for late arrival. I arrived in Ohio at 8:00 o'clock that night and they had a smoking room with two single beds reserved for me. I asked how that could be and they explained, "Because that's what you asked for."

My goal was to get through just one week without someone dropping the ball at my expense. I found that I couldn't get through one day without this happening. I quickly gave up on the journal because it was so depressing.

Being Less Than Outstanding at Certain Tasks Is Okay but Being Incompetent Isn't

I can't change people's incompetence as a consumer but I can choose to spend my money elsewhere. This is one reason incompetence is expensive for employers. Employers know that it's a better financial decision to lose an incompetent employee than to lose a customer. Another reason incompetence is expensive is because it results in having to redo work and missing deadlines.

Bob in Wisconsin had a reputation for attention to detail. Whenever his boss asked him to do a project, Bob would respond, "Do you only want a good job, or do you want a Bob job?" Your work doesn't have to be as outstanding as Bob's as long as you're consistently proficient and accurate. Highly valued employees aren't necessarily the fastest or best but can be trusted to consistently do the job well. They are professionals who can be trusted to do a solid job no matter what the task may be. You'll be on track to becoming a highly valued employee when you earn a reputation for always doing your job accurately and thoroughly.

Professionalism Means Doing Your Best Even When You Don't Feel Like It

Being competent at what you do is the first quality of a professional. The second is always giving your best effort. People in show business know the show must go on if their career is to go on. Legendary magician Harry Houdini did his last magic show in 1926 in such excruciating pain from a burst appendix that he collapsed on stage and died in the hospital the next week. This isn't to suggest that you endanger your health in order to do your job. However, too many people allow the slightest excuse to become a reason not to do their best work. It then becomes all too easy to form bad habits that can follow throughout an entire career. It's much easier not to form a bad habit in the first place than to try to break it years later.

Houdini's work ethic wasn't unique to his era. Exactly 50 years later in 1976, the members of Fleetwood Mac experienced turmoil in their personal lives. Keyboardist Christine McVie was going through a bitter divorce from bass player John McVie. Singer Stevie Nicks was going through a bitter separation from her long-time companion and guitarist Lindsey Buckingham. Drummer Mick Fleetwood was divorcing his wife. Despite their tumultuous personal lives, they pulled together and recorded "Rumours." It went on to become their best-selling album and defined their career. This level of professionalism isn't limited to superstars. Even those who are trying to ramp up their careers have to exhibit the same level of dedication. Actress Christina Applegate is best known for her role as Kelly Bundy in the 1987 to 1997 Fox television show *Married with Children*. She broke her ankle while playing the lead role in the Broadway play *Sweet Charity* in 2005 but finished the show despite excruciating pain. This show of professionalism soon had her on the talk shows and helped bring her back into the show business spotlight.

> The best employees don't necessarily have to be the brightest or smartest. They need to have a positive attitude and leave their personal problems at home.
>
> Laura Toddie, Heritage Pet Hospital,
> Rochester, Minnesota

Leave Your Home Life at Home

Your personal habits must be as professional as your work habits. Another sign of a professional is what he or she talks about. Few things are more annoying to coworkers and managers than to hear the soap opera of people's home lives. Work is a place to make a living, not to go for therapy. People may lend a sympathetic ear when you tell them about your personal problems but inside they want to scream "Enough already! I've got problems of my own. I don't need to hear about yours, too." Don't fall for the hype when companies claim their employees are one big family. This isn't true. You are people bound by a paycheck. Even if you have developed personal friendships with coworkers, friendship officially begins when the workday ends.

One woman told me that she didn't have time to spend with coworkers after work because she had to pick up her kids, make dinner, and then do housework. She explained that work was the only convenient time and place to discuss her marital problems. I hoped she was kidding but she wasn't. I suggested that she go to lunch with coworkers and discuss personal problems on personal time. She explained that they didn't like to hear about her personal problems during their lunch break. I couldn't believe she was serious. She clearly saw her job as something to serve her and not the other way around.

Professionalism also applies to what you talk about in front of customers. I was at a Nashville restaurant in March 2005 when the server asked how I was doing. I gave my standard response, "Better than I deserve! How are you?" He explained that he wasn't doing well because he was having trouble with his finances and was worried about the health of Pope John Paul II. The entertainment experience of eating out had just been reduced to zero for this meal. It was naive of him to answer a rhetorical question. I might have felt a little empathy or at least identified with him if he told me he was worried that the Tennessee Titans might lose our starting quarterback or that lawmakers were trying to pass a state income tax again. The problem with his response regarding the Pope was that he was already on his deathbed and everyone knew it. It was sad but I came to the restaurant to be happy. The server just didn't get that. The ironic part was the comment about his finances. Tips are how servers make most of their income and I'm a generous tipper. He would have received a better tip from me than from most of his customers if he had just been a run-of-the-mill server. Whining about his finances hurt them even more by ensuring that he was getting a minimum tip from me no matter how good his service was. This turned out to be a moot point since he was as unprofessional in his service as he was in his behavior.

A good employee will leave his or her drama at home.

Amy Dabney, Realty Executives Associates,
Knoxville, Tennessee

Respect Other People's Values Even When You Don't Agree with Them

How a professional talks is as important as what he or she talks about. We all have the right to speak freely from a legal standpoint but don't have the right to speak freely from a social standpoint. We live in a politically correct world where it has almost become impossible to say anything without someone being offended. Most of us don't intend to offend and wouldn't if we just knew what we weren't supposed to say. The terms are changing so fast that it's hard to keep up with them. Professional Secretaries Day was officially renamed Administrative Professionals Day in 2000. Many companies now call their employees associates. Waitresses and waiters are now servers. Ethnic communities are also changing their preferred terms. "Hispanic" is usually preferred over "Latino." "Negro" was replaced with "colored people," then "black," and now "African American." Martin Luther King Jr. preferred "Negro" to "black" because he felt that "black" denoted a more militant faction of the civil rights movement. Today "black" is far more acceptable than "Negro."

Keeping up with all the terms is a nuisance no matter what your job title, cultural heritage, or social beliefs may be. None of us likes having to constantly relearn the language. Yet, this is exactly what professionals do. It's not important that you use the correct term every time. It's important that you try to respect other people's values even when you don't agree with them. Part of American Express's Code of Conduct reads:

You are expected to treat your colleagues . . . with respect and dignity. The Company expects leaders to seek out the ideas of subordinates and to involve them in decisions whenever appropriate. At the same time, once a decision is made, everyone is expected to pull together and support it.

Learn How to Disagree without Being Insubordinate

You must also learn how to disagree with people without being disrespectful. Nowhere is this more important than when you disagree with your boss. It's okay to voice your opinion in the right place, time, and manner. Being able to form your own opinions is a sign of being an adult. Knowing when to keep them to yourself is a sign of maturity and professionalism. Intel Corporation actually encourages its employees to disagree as long as there are no personal attacks. Colin Powell adamantly disagreed with President Bush about how to proceed in Iraq when he served as Secretary of State. He still followed his boss's orders and served as the president's advocate. Colin Powell was a highly valued employee. It's no surprise that both the Republicans and Democrats heavily courted him to run for office on their tickets.

Thom Wright had worked in human resources for the State of North Carolina for over 20 years when State Attorney General Mike Easley interviewed him for the position of Human Resources Director with the state's Department of Justice. When Mr. Easley asked Thom why he should be appointed to the position, Thom responded, "If you're looking for a yes-man, I'm not your guy. What I will do is give you options and keep you out of hot water." Thom got the job. When Attorney General Easley decided to run for higher office, he looked to Thom to step up to a higher position. Mr. Easley went on to become North Carolina's 72nd governor and Thom rose to Director of the Office of State Personnel, the highest-ranking human resources job in the state. Thom told me he agrees with the governor about 99 percent of the time, but respects the governor and does what his boss tells him to do 100 percent of the time.

Dress for the Job You Want, Not the Job You Have

Small choices you make on a daily basis will define you. Professionals have a habit of making good choices. One of those choices is how they dress. Managers constantly tell me they're amazed at how applicants will dress for job interviews. Young men show up looking like they just crawled out of bed wearing baggy jeans pulled down to reveal their boxer shorts, a baseball cap turned sideways, and three-day stubble. Young women show up wearing miniskirts and sandals. Others wear low-rise jeans, flip flops, spaghetti strap tops with no bra, and expose their midriff. Both adorn their look with unlimited tattoos and facial piercings. I'm constantly amazed at how people will dress for work or job interviews. Thom Wright summed it up best when he said, "If you would wear it to the state fair, then don't wear it to work!"

In deciding how you should dress to be considered a highly valued employee, first see if your company has a dress code. Dress codes tell you how you shouldn't dress. To see how you should dress, emulate your boss. Even if it isn't possible to emulate your boss exactly, he or she will provide good cues on how you should dress. Notice his or her shoes, hair, and jewelry. Does your boss always wear his shirts heavily starched? Does she wear jewelry? How much skin does he or she show?

The director at one university told me they held a career class for GED students who were trying to leave welfare and get jobs. They brought in a professional businesswoman who showed them how to dress. The class went so ballistic over someone telling them what they couldn't wear that the director had to threaten to call campus security. This is unfortunate because those women needed to know what is going to be expected of them in the business world. People do judge a book by the cover.

Make your choices carefully because you will eventually have to deal with the consequences.

Cheryl Callighan, EOffice-Virtual Assistants,
Denver, Colorado

Associate with Other Highly Valued Employees

Another good choice professionals make is who they hang out with at work. The people you surround yourself with will have a huge impact on who you become. You will internalize their values, standards, and work ethic. There are cliques at work, both healthy and unhealthy. Avoid the unhealthy cliques. These are the ones who gossip about everyone, constantly badmouth the boss behind his or her back, and mutiny by ambushing the boss as a group. They constantly try to recruit more employees to join their ranks because their strength comes from their numbers. One manager learned how quickly this can happen when her toxic group invited a new hire to lunch with them. She said, "I was amazed at how they turned a good employee into one of them in less than an hour. It was almost as if she had been bitten by a vampire."

I once saw a bumper sticker that said it's hard to soar with the eagles when you're surrounded by turkeys. While it's wrong to blame others for our own lack of accomplishment, it's easier to succeed when we're surrounded by others who succeed. This is why groups ranging from those trying to lose weight to those trying to overcome alcoholism assign accountability partners. You'd have no difficulty being at your best every day if you worked in an office with Donald Trump, Bill Gates, and Rudy Giuliani. It will be much more difficult when you work around people who dress like slouches, curse like sailors, and have as much company spirit as the cartoon character *Dilbert*.

> Be careful the environment you choose for it will shape you; be careful the friends you choose for you will become like them.
>
> W. Clement Stone

Conclusion

Be a professional regardless of whether you work on Broadway in New York City or Broad Street in small town America. This means incompetence is not an option and you always do your best work, even when you don't feel like it. This also means you should surround yourself with the right people. Birds of a feather flock together, so surround yourself with other highly valued employees.

CHAPTER 13

Check Your Ego at the Door

At Microsoft there are lots of brilliant ideas, but the image is that they all come from the top—I'm afraid that's not quite right.

Bill Gates

Singer Harry Belafonte was inspired to create a recording project to raise money for famine victims in Ethiopia in 1985. This presented a major challenge to legendary producer Quincy Jones who had the unenviable task of gathering 21 of the most popular stars of the time into one room. The music tracks were recorded beforehand and Jones decided to record the vocals on the night of the American Music Awards when all the stars would be together. He sent each one a tape ahead of time with a note that read, "Check your ego at the door." He had Al Jarreau, Billy Joel, Bob Dylan, Bruce Springsteen, Cyndi Lauper, Dan Akroyd, Daryl Hall, Diana Ross, Dionne Warwick, Huey Lewis, James Ingram, Kenny Loggins, Kenny Rogers, Kim Carnes, Lionel Richie, Michael Jackson, Paul Simon, Ray Charles, Steve Perry, Stevie Wonder, Tina Turner, and Willie Nelson in one room at the A&M Records studio in Hollywood. The session went off without a hitch and "We Are the World" sold

800,000 copies its first week. It was the highest debuting single since John Lennon's "Imagine," the fastest rising since Elton John's "Island Girl," and won Grammy Awards for Song of the Year and Record of the Year. Each of the stars who participated in the project was more than cooperative. This wasn't because they didn't have big egos. Some of them were known for having big egos and not being the easiest to work with. What made the event go so well was that each one knew the night was about something bigger than themselves. They knew when to step out of the spotlight and blend into the woodwork.

The Incredible Power of Gratitude

It feels good to give but it feels better to give and be appreciated. People will do anything for you when they feel appreciated. It feels awful to give and feel unappreciated. We feel slighted when this happens and the feelings can sometimes turn into bitterness or resentment. I've held this discussion with numerous people. Some suggest that if you give with the expectation of getting something in return, you're giving for the wrong reason and should discontinue giving. This is only half true. You shouldn't give for the wrong reason. Giving to get something in return isn't giving; it's manipulation. We still expect one thing in return when we give—a gesture of gratitude. Showing gratitude for someone else's kindness or generosity is proper etiquette.

Imagine that you're sitting in a traffic jam on the interstate. The motorist next to you indicates that he wants to merge into your lane. You wave him in, he merges, and then continues on without any acknowledgment. He doesn't owe you anything. He asked to come into your lane and you chose to let him in. It would have still been common courtesy for him to make a gesture of thanks. This minor incident can change your whole attitude in a negative way. You'll probably be less likely to let in the next motorist who asks to cut in front of you. While a lack of good manners and an increase in rudeness don't justify a motorist pulling out a gun when he becomes angry, they might help explain why road rage is becoming so much more common.

Now let's look at how your attitude can be changed in a positive way with the simplest gesture of gratitude. Let the driver of a tractor trailer merge into your lane and then watch what he does. He'll flash his taillights to thank you. Drivers are taught to do this in driving school. They act professionally behind the wheel just as Fleetwood Mac acted professionally when recording "Rumours." Notice how this one small gesture of gratitude from one individual can influence how you treat others. You'll probably be more likely to let in the next driver who asks to cut in front of you because the previous one treated you so respectfully.

I teach managers to treat employees consistently regardless of their personalities. Yet, it's impossible to completely rise above human instincts. Managers are more likely to give raises and promotions to employees they like than those they don't like. Managers like employees who are grateful for what they get and dislike those who think they're entitled to something.

The benefit of gratitude in business relationships isn't limited to employer-employee relationships. It also applies to customers. Arielle Ford spent 15 years representing Deepak Chopra as his publicist. She admits that she worked harder and more passionately for Dr. Chopra than for some of her other clients because he showed her so much gratitude. He regularly sent her flowers and occasionally sent bonus checks to thank her for a job well done. Mark Victor Hansen and Jack Canfield also sent her flowers and constantly showed their gratitude for her work on the *Chicken Soup for the Soul* series. It comes as no surprise that these three authors have been enormously successful in their careers.

I'm constantly reminded of how much influence other people's gratitude has on me in my business life. Pastors who pay to attend my seminars aren't charged for my books. They always thank me when I give them a book but less than 3 percent ever follow up with a thank-you note or e-mail. One who did was Eddie Brittain of Cherokee Church in Johnson City, Tennessee. Eddie is one very impressive individual who excels at whatever he does. This isn't just because of his job skills. It's because he is such a professional that he is inspiring to be around. He attended a management seminar I gave in Virginia in March 2005. I gave him a complimentary copy of one of my books and he promptly followed up with a thank-you e-mail. Later, I asked him to review a new book I had just finished and write an endorsement if he felt it was appropriate. He was the first to respond out of the 10 people I asked. This placed him on the top of my list. Later that year, he contacted me with a request for consulting. It was at that point that I realized how much of an impact Eddie's professionalism had on me. My job is helping people solve business problems and I love what I do. I'm also human and get tired. There are days when I spend 12 hours or more listening to people's problems and I'm not exactly pumped up about returning a phone call to listen to yet another. The situation was remarkably different when I returned Eddie's call. Not only was I more than willing to call and talk to him but also I looked forward to the conversation. His level of professionalism made me feel good about what I do and want to do a better job at it. Eddie doesn't behave professionally to get something in return. Yet, being such a professional gives him an incredible advantage in his career. When people like you so much that they want to help you, your job future is as bright as it can be.

I'm constantly reminded of how much influence other people's gratitude has on me in my personal life as well. Last year I decided to donate my old mini van to someone in need. I found a single mom who was taking care of her elderly parents as well as her own kids. I could think of no better place for my old Chevy to go and happily presented her with the keys, then never heard from her again. A little voice inside me said, "You'd think someone would take 30 seconds to send a thank-you note for such a generous gift." I had to make myself promise not to let that experience influence my decision the next time I think about donating a vehicle to a charitable cause. It's so much easier to be generous with people when they show even the slightest gesture of gratitude.

Show Your Gratitude First, and the Money Will Come Later

I often hear employees at restaurants and retail stores complain, "They don't pay me enough to do this job." I ask if they honestly believe more money would change their performance. Most claim they would do a better job if they were paid more. I then ask if they're grateful for the money they already earn. Most won't directly answer yes or no. They instead argue that they would start being grateful once they get more money.

We've all heard it said that people who can't be happy when they're single won't be happy when they're married, people who can't be happy when they're poor won't be happy when they're rich, and so on. If you've ever known someone who was in an unhappy marriage, you'll remember how sure he or she was that eternal bliss would begin the day the divorce decree was issued. You'll also remember that didn't happen and eventually some level of loneliness and depression set in. There was some value to the companionship that wasn't appreciated until he or she was alone, no matter how much he or she may have resented the former spouse. Many people are so busy lusting for grass they think is greener on the other side of the fence that they don't appreciate what they have until it's gone.

Money is another example. Most people believe that having more money would make them happier but it can actually be the worst thing that can happen. For example, lottery winners have a higher rate of bankruptcy and divorce than nonlottery winners do. The problem isn't money or marital status; it's that people are making their happiness contingent on outside events they have little control over. Failing to take responsibility for your own happiness is the surest way to be unhappy because it leads to a victim mentality. This can be compounded by an entitlement mentality when people feel they've been denied something they're entitled to have. This is why I always answer "How are you today?" with "Better than I deserve!" I ask people who say they deserve to be happy *why* they deserve it. No one has ever come up with a satisfactory reason. Life doesn't come with a satisfaction guarantee or your money back. We all have the option of being happy but happiness isn't an entitlement or a result of any event. It's a choice. I find it ironic that those who say they deserve to be happy are the least happy people I know. Those who consider everything they receive to be a gift or blessing that they appreciate are the happiest people I know.

Show gratitude for your job and a predictable cycle will occur. People value their job more when they're grateful for it. When people value a job, they do it well. When they do it well, they get promoted and make more money. When they're not grateful for their jobs, they don't value them and don't do them well. They then stay stuck in a job they hate, complain about how they aren't paid enough to do the job, and whine about how they deserve more. You won't be grateful for what you get in the future if you're not grateful for what you have now.

Failing to be grateful for what we have prevents us from getting more. It can also cause us to lose what we already have. People are only grateful for things they value. Things that are valued are taken care of, while things that aren't valued get neglected. Neglecting something causes it to deteriorate until it's ultimately lost. This applies to everything from relationships to health to jobs. One reason so many people take things for granted is because of the high standard of living discussed in Chapter 7. This has resulted in an entitlement mentality for many. When people think they're entitled to something, they don't appreciate it when they get it. They take it for granted because they truly believe it should be granted to them.

Conclusion

Being proud of what you do is important but being too proud of yourself can lead to arrogance and arrogance can kill a career. Be proud of what you do while remaining humble enough to be grateful for your job. Show gratitude and never, ever take your job for granted.

CHAPTER 14

Take Charge of Your Own Destiny

Without continual growth and progress, such words as improvement, achievement, and success have no meaning.

Benjamin Franklin

Albert Einstein said that we only use 10 percent of our brains. Dale Carnegie believed we use 15 percent. Most of the psychological community today believes that people use 100 percent of our brains but agree that few of us ever achieve our full capacity to succeed.

Managers study something called the Peter Principle. This states that people get promoted to their level of incompetence. The good part about this is that people get to discover their skill sets and limitations. The bad part is that we don't know what we're really capable of until we reach our limit, and most never reach it.

Make Your Intentions Known

One of my personal pet peeves is motorists in busy intersections who don't use their turn signals. I often find myself on the opposite side attempting to guess if they intend to turn left, right, or go straight. It's important for motorists to make their intentions known in order to safely get to where they want to go. It's also important for you to make your intentions known to get to where you want to go with your career. The first step to succeeding at anything is making the decision. The second step is announcing your intentions. Announcing your intentions accomplishes two important goals. It creates expectations of you in others and it creates expectations of you in yourself. You dramatically increase your chances of success when everyone is expecting you to succeed.

This is what Carl from New York did. He was in his early twenties and attended my management seminar at the University of Pittsburgh last year. He visited my web site prior to attending the seminar and read about the *Excellence in Management Award* I present to managers who exhibit extraordinary talent. He came up to introduce himself at break and said, "I want you to know that I'm going to win the *Excellence in Management Award* next year. I'm going to be one of those young managers like Katy in Georgia or Susan in Massachusetts who reaffirm your hope in the next generation." If we hadn't held this conversation and Carl then wins the award in the future, I would have been neither surprised nor confirmed in my perception of him. Now that he has created an expectation in me that he is going to win, I would be surprised if he doesn't win.

I send a follow-up e-mail to each attendee thanking him or her for attending the seminar. Carl replied and reminded me that he would win the award. He's determined to succeed and he will, but at far more than winning an award. He will succeed in his career because he's doing all the right things.

Actor Jim Carey did something similar. He wrote himself a check for $10 million when he was a struggling actor and kept it in his wallet until he could actually cash it. He took it out and looked at it constantly to remind himself of his goal. I copied his method last year after reading a story about Marcus Buckingham. He's the author of *The One Thing You Need to Know*[1] and co-author of *First, Break All the Rules*[2] and *Now, Discover Your Strengths*.[3] He makes $55,000 per speech. I made up a mock check to myself for $55,000 and filled out the memo line with "speaking fee." I carry it in my wallet and look at it when I need motivation. I'm a long way from reaching that goal and the odds are probably a million to one that I will ever reach that point, but that little piece of paper creates an expectation in me. Now writing about that goal in a book that thousands of people will read has created an expectation in others and a level of accountability I never imagined. Carl and I are at different stages in our careers but the benefit of announcing our intentions is equal for both of us.

Announcing your goals increases your chances of succeeding at everything from careers to losing weight. Certainly telling someone you're going to lose weight won't physically help you shed the pounds. It will help you stay mentally and emotionally focused on doing what needs to be done to lose the weight. Sharing your goals with someone isn't the key to succeeding; it's an indicator of how committed you are. Demonstrate your commitment to your own career success by letting people know that you intend to become indispensable to your employer.

Your Raise Will Become Effective When You Become More Effective

Your company wants you to earn a raise. A woman from New Jersey argued, "My company doesn't want to give me a raise." I agreed. Her company doesn't want to *give* her a raise; they want her to *earn* it. The worst thing an employee can do to himself is ask the company to "give" him a raise. This is a welfare mentality. Companies cannot give raises because raises aren't handouts. They're rewards that must be earned. The National Football League doesn't give away the Lombardi trophy to a team they feel has been the most loyal or has the best team spirit. The trophy is awarded to the team who earns it by winning the Superbowl.

Companies want employees to get raises, but only as a reward for hard work and not as an entitlement. They don't want freeloaders who expect more money just because they need it. The lowly valued employee who hasn't increased his value to the company but sticks his hand out and says, "I want a raise just because I've been here for another year" is a thorn in the employer's side. The owner of a chain of retail stores in Nebraska told me his store managers make about $40,000 a year but he wants them to make $60,000 a year. It wouldn't cost him a dime to pay the extra $20,000 because they work on a bonus system and would be making the company more money. He was frustrated that they don't want to make the extra money. They're content to make $40,000 while whining that they don't make more. Run-of-the-mill employees and lowly valued employees ask companies to give them raises. Highly valued employees ask "What do I need to do to *earn* a raise?" Heather in Iowa confirmed how well this principle works. She sent me the following e-mail after seeking my advice:

> Glenn, I got the restaurant manager position!!! Thank you for your help and coaching in the hiring process. I greatly appreciate it. I said what you told me to say in the interview: What can I do to *earn* the position? Once I said that, the interviewer said 'I don't need to ask you any more questions. You got the job.' Excellent. Also the pay raise is awesome—$10,000! Can you believe it? Thank you again for everything!

Conclusion

Your company can give you an opportunity but can't give you success. They want you to be a highly valued employee and only you can make that happen. Your destiny is in your own hands. Highly valued employees take responsibility for their own advancement and create the truest form of job security by becoming indispensable to their companies.

CHAPTER 15

Don't Confuse Education with Knowledge

It is a thousand times better to have common sense without education than to have education without common sense.

Robert Green Ingersoll

Government statistics indicate approximately three million college students are over age 35. They also reveal that holders of bachelor's degrees earn approximately 60 percent more than those with only a high school diploma. What they don't reveal is that a college degree can be helpful in qualifying for a job but often has little benefit after getting a job. Thousands of mid-career adults are wasting their time, effort, and money hoping a degree will give them a career boost. Many are making the mistake of looking to someone else to give them a helping hand when what they really need to do is help themselves by improving their work habits.

Going back to college is badly overhyped as the magic pill to instantly jump-start careers. One reason for this is that college for mid-career adults has become big business. Every major city is brimming with advertisements from nontraditional colleges on billboards, television, radio, the Internet, in newspapers, and even flyers on telephone poles. Notice how many of these colleges are located in office parks and shopping centers. Furthering a formal education can be beneficial for some but many of these institutions are selling false hope. Their so-called counselors are often nothing more than sales reps who are paid a commission to recruit new students, even when it's not in the student's best interest. Their claims of what their certificate or degree will do for a graduate's earning potential aren't realistic and it's nothing but a rip-off for many students. It has gotten so out of control that the federal government has shut some of these colleges down.

There's nothing wrong with going back to college as long as it's done for the right reasons and people are realistic about their expectations. I admire people who go to college at night while working during the day. The situation can change when people stop working in order to attend college. On the surface, it sounds good to say you are going back to college. In reality, many are using college as an excuse to avoid work or avoid working at a "real" job. Most claim they're working hard at furthering their education to further their careers. This is probably true for those who are studying specific career disciplines but can be a load of garbage for others. Many are piddling around by taking useless classes and making no progress toward anything. We see this in the growing number of students who spend six years or more attending a two-year junior college and still haven't graduated. We also see this with the results once they do graduate. These degrees often have little impact on earnings.

Another problem with interrupting a career for college is that many people don't count all the costs. In my experience, few people realize the true price they pay when they put a career on hold to attend college. Imagine that a mid-career adult with 25 years left to retirement leaves a $30,000-a-year job and goes back to college for three years. He spends $15,000 getting a degree, but will pay far more than $15,000 for it. There's also the $90,000 of income he forfeited by not working for three years. There's also the lost savings for retirement. He would have put $13,500 into his retirement account if he worked and saved 15 percent of his income for each of those three years. This money would have seen about a 12 percent annual growth rate if he invested it in good growth stock mutual funds. This means the $13,500 would have grown to $216,000 by retirement. Now let's calculate the true cost of the three years he took out of his career to get the degree:

Tuition and books:	$15,000
Lost income:	$90,000
Lost retirement saving:	$216,000
True cost of the degree	$321,000

He'd have to earn nearly $13,000 more per year for the next 25 years to cover the true cost of getting the degree. This may happen for some but won't for many. In 48 *Days to the Work You Love,*[1] career coach Dan Miller says that 85 percent of the reason people get promoted is due to personal skills and only 15 percent is attributed to training or formal education. Many employers aren't looking for formal education because so much of it is irrelevant to the real world.

> When a subject becomes totally obsolete, we make it a required course.
>
> Peter Drucker

Why College Degrees Don't Necessarily Increase Job Skills

Another problem with going back to college is that a college degree sometimes doesn't increase people's useful job skills. Even useful skills that are being taught in many colleges could easily be learned at work. For example, thousands of college students are taking classes to learn computer programs such as Microsoft Word. Word is the dominant word processing program in the market today and has become the de facto standard.

Competency in using Word is certainly a useful job skill. However, the majority of Word's users never use the majority of its features. Most companies only use its basic functions and are willing to teach employees who are willing to learn. Even if your employer won't teach you, it's still not necessary to attend college to learn this skill. Microsoft provides an extensive free tutorial that anyone can take using any personal computer with an Internet connection.

Other skills that colleges are teaching can be irrelevant to many people's careers. For example, thousands of students take classes on how to use Microsoft PowerPoint. This is an excellent program but taking a college class on how to use it is a waste for most people. The average individual can learn to use PowerPoint in less than an hour by taking the built-in, free tutorial. It's much easier to use than Word and is probably the simplest Microsoft program to learn. Even the most inept computer user could sufficiently master this program in a day. Taking an entire semester for this is ridiculous. The second reason taking a class on how to use PowerPoint is a waste for most people is because very few will ever use it at work. It's a multimedia presentation program and most people don't need to make multimedia presentations to do their jobs. I've spoken at over 150 colleges in 25 states over the past 10 years and never used PowerPoint until I did a teleseminar for Thompson Interactive in Washington, DC, in May 2005. Thompson works with top human resource experts and law firms all over the country and PowerPoint is the perfect tool to link everyone. Callers from California to New York were able to follow my presentation online using PowerPoint. It was absolutely perfect for that situation, but most people will never do an online presentation for companies from coast to coast.

Dave Ramsey put it best when he said, "A college degree is often nothing more than a pedigree. I don't want to know where you got your degree. I want to know what you learned while you were getting it and how it's going to benefit me as an employer." Dave is certainly qualified to make this statement. He's the author of *New York Times* best sellers *Financial Peace*[2] and *The Total Money Makeover*,[3] a self-made multimillionaire, nationally syndicated radio talk show host, and owner of a company with over 100 employees.

Brendan Keegan is the executive vice president of human resources for Marriott International. He reports directly to Bill Marriott Jr., whose company now employs over 150,000 people worldwide.

Brendan had been with Marriott for 33 years at the time I interviewed him. We discussed the value of an education and he explained that Marriott hires 400 to 600 new college graduates for entry-level management training positions each year. He also explained that education isn't limited to college. Marriot offers a nationally acclaimed program called "Pathways to Independence" to teach skills to welfare recipients and help move them into the workforce. Half the program teaches job skills and the other half teaches basic life skills such as how to open a bank account. Marriott is willing to teach individuals how to become a housekeeper and how to become an employee, but only if they're willing to learn and work hard. Those who are willing to work hard have a bright future with Marriott and also have the opportunity to move into management.

Education's purpose is to replace an empty mind with an open one.

Malcolm Forbes

Why a College Degree Alone Won't Make You a Highly Valued Employee

College degrees don't even make people highly valued employees in fields that require extensive education. Imagine that you're a heart surgeon. You hold a Bachelor of Science degree in biology from an Ivy League college. You graduated at the top of your class (summa cum laude). You hold a medical degree from another Ivy League college. You graduated second in your class (magna cum laude) from medical school. Now imagine that you're applying for a job opening in your hospital for head of cardiac surgery. The hospital's board of directors has narrowed its decision down to you and one other applicant. The other applicant's resume is nearly identical to yours. You both make $750,000 a year. You've both been practicing surgery for 10 years. She also graduated summa cum laude from an Ivy League college with a Bachelor of Science degree in biology. She went to medical school with you and graduated one position behind you. Do you think the board will choose you over her because you graduated higher in your class? If you do, think again. The board might have chosen you over her if they were hiring you straight out of medical school. Your academic record was more significant at that early point in your career because it was the best indicator of how well you were likely to perform in the real word.

You now have a 10-year track record at work. How well you performed as a student is far less important than how well you performed as an employee in the real world. Notice that I didn't say, "How you performed as a surgeon in the real world." You now have a 10-year track record of how well you performed as a surgeon inside the operating room and as an employee outside the operating room. Even a perfect record in surgery won't be enough to get you the position of department head. What you did outside the operating room for the past 10 years will now come into play.

Conclusion

This purpose of this chapter isn't to diminish the value of a college education; it's to clarify it. Getting a college education can be good as long as it's not used as a substitute for hard work, you can afford it, and your expectations are realistic. Most employers look to today's entry-level workers to be tomorrow's managers. UPS prefers executives who once drove one of their brown trucks. They make it clear that there's no career fast track in their organization. Regardless of education, it requires dedication and persistence to climb the UPS corporate ladder.

Many companies will even pay tuition for employees who attend college while they work. Others don't even require college degrees to be promoted. A district manager for a Wendy's franchise told me that it's possible for someone without a college degree to start as a cook and end up as a manager in about 24 months. She shared the story of a single mom who once struggled to feed her kids and ended up making $70,000 a year in a district manager's position. "Wow!" I said. "I guess you have lots of single moms wanting to come work for you and climb the company ladder." She explained this wasn't the case because 99 percent of the people she encountered weren't willing to work hard enough to make that happen.

Most of the large companies that I interviewed for this book have education requirements for upper level positions. Nearly every one has made exceptions for highly motivated individuals who lacked the academic credentials normally required for a position. None has ever made an exception for individuals who weren't willing to work hard.

CHAPTER 16

Avoid Learned Helplessness

Learned helplessness is the giving-up reaction, the quitting response that follows from the belief that whatever you do doesn't matter.

Arnold Schwarzenegger

Notice that the title of this chapter isn't "Avoid Learned Power-lessness." We always have some power in even the most dire of circumstances. This was the case of Victor Frankl. He was interred in a Nazi concentration camp during World War II where prisoners were executed or starved to death. He was subjected to experiments so horrendous that they're unspeakable. He observed that people who survived maintained power over their minds even when their bodies were ravaged. Those who gave up in their minds were soon dead. He later wrote of his observations in *Man's Search for Meaning*.[1]

Most people will never be put in dire circumstances like Dr. Frankl. We live in a land of limitless opportunities that most people throughout the history of the world only dreamed of. Yet, our country today is full of people who believe they are powerless. They've developed a learned helplessness. Dale Carnegie wrote in *How to Win*

Friends and Influence People[2] that the one thing people want more than anything is to feel important. Traditionally, people have sought to feel important by being loved, admired, or accomplishing something. Many people today seek to feel important by being pitied. We've become a society of whiny victims.

> The last freedom is choosing your attitude.
>
> Victor Frankl

Life's Unfair—Get Over It

I meet about 10,000 people every year in my seminars. This allows me the opportunity to gauge firsthand what America is thinking and how we feel about ourselves. I've been blessed to meet some of the most inspirational and impressive individuals in the world. I've also seen humanity at its worst. I'm amazed at how consistent the trend is. It seems that the less people have to complain or feel self-pity about, the more they do. The ones who have the most reason to feel sorry for themselves are the ones who never do. Here are the stories of three of the most inspiring individuals I've met.

The Harley Riding Hair Stylist Who Never Says Never

I met Robyn Flynn when she attended a seminar I gave at Miami University. She rides a Harley Davidson and is living proof that dynamite comes in small packages. She's vivacious, incredibly upbeat, and inspiring to be around. She also has plenty of reason not to be.

She and her 11-year-old son Austin had just returned from a trip to New York City when an unexpected event turned her life upside down. It was a special trip for Austin, who was born with muscular dystrophy. MD made it impossible for him to do the most basic tasks such as tying his shoes, eating, or going to the bathroom without assistance. He got to meet Justin Timberlake while in New York and was on top of the world. They returned home to Ohio on Monday and Austin began junior high school on Tuesday. Robyn received the fateful phone call from the hospital on Wednesday. She arrived at the hospital to find nurses performing CPR on Austin's dad. She screamed at the doctors, "No! You cannot let this man die! We have a little boy with special needs and he needs his father. Don't give up on him! He has to live. He just has to!" He didn't. Robyn found herself facing the task of raising a child with special needs without his father.

Austin's needs required Robyn to miss time at work. This would not have been as much of a challenge if she was only a hair stylist, but she faced an even more daunting proposition. She also owned the salon. As discussed in Chapter 6, business owners work more hours than their employees. Now Robyn had to find a way to work less while making more money. If necessity is the mother of invention, then Robyn became the most inventive salon owner I've ever met. She devised a plan to ensure that the salon almost ran itself and generated a consistent monthly income by scheduling all her clients a year in advance. This allowed her to be out of the salon when she needed to be and also increased her income. She became so successful that she now teaches seminars to help other salon owners all across the country make their businesses more profitable. She chose to control her circumstances instead of letting her circumstances control her.

There's More to Alvin Law Than What's Missing

I met Alvin Law at the National Speakers Association annual meeting in Atlanta in July 2005. About 1,500 people were eating dinner in a large banquet hall when I noticed him a few tables over. What first caught my attention was that he had a wristwatch on his ankle. Then I saw him put his feet on the table and thought that was rude. Next he picked up a glass of wine with his foot and I realized he had no arms. I watched for a few minutes while debating whether it would be impolite to ask about his disability. My first shallow thought was, "Do I shake his foot?" Then I thought to myself, "You're not a 6-year old. Go meet the man." I did and his story changed my whole perspective on life. Alvin has less sympathy for himself, anger toward others, and bitterness than anyone I've ever met. In fact, he has none of the above. Yet, he probably has more reason to feel these unhealthy emotions than anyone I know.

He was born with no arms in 1960 in rural Saskatchewan, Canada. His birth mother used a drug called Thalidomide while pregnant with him. The story of Thalidomide is the first reason he could easily be bitter. Many people in post-World War II Europe had trouble sleeping due to what is now known as Post Traumatic Stress Disorder. Sleeping pills in the 1950s were often addictive and people could overdose. Pharmaceutical companies marketed Thalidomide as the first nonbarbiturate sleeping pill and one that had no side effects. Drug testing in those days was done very differently than it is today. Canadian doctors who were chosen to participate in studies were labeled "qualified investigators." They administered unproven drugs to the general public and reported the results to the drugs' makers. Pregnant women taking Thalidomide reported that it eliminated morning sickness and pharmaceutical companies soon began marketing it as a morning sickness drug. They advertised that it was safe for pregnant women even though they had not tested it to see if this was true. Alvin's mother's doctor gave her free samples of Thalidomide to help with her morning sickness and Alvin paid the price. Thalidomide was finally banned in 1963. At least 1,300 cases where Thalidomide babies were born with various deformities have been documented. This is the second reason Alvin could easily be bitter. He told me he has met numerous other people whose mothers used Thalidomide. Many were born with missing fingers, hands, or feet, but Alvin was born missing both of his arms.

The next reason Alvin could easily feel bitterness or anger is because of what his birth family did after he was born. They lived on a farm owned by his grandmother, who was an extremely superstitious woman with some ancient beliefs. She thought Alvin's lack of arms was a sign from Satan and threatened to kick his parents off the farm if they brought him home. She believed the crops would dry up and locusts would swarm if he came to live with them, so his birth parents gave him to the government when he was only two weeks old. The government then placed him in a foster home with a 53-year-old foster dad and 55-year-old foster mom. They were told he would only be there for a few weeks but ended up raising him to adulthood. Still, it wasn't love at first sight. His foster dad didn't want him and Alvin says his foster mom describes him as the ugliest baby she ever saw. She says she took him in only because ugly babies need love, too.

They still weren't allowed to legally adopt him because he was an official ward of the government. The government paid for his rehabilitation for 12 years and even provided prosthetic arms. The problem was that Alvin didn't want prosthetic arms. By age 16, he had learned to get along quite well by using his feet. He refused to wear the prosthetic arms and the Saskatchewan government threatened to take him away from his foster parents if he didn't. Instead of getting angry, he turned the situation into an opportunity. He told the government that if they wanted to pay for something, it should be something of real worth, and convinced them to pay for his college education instead.

Alvin went on to a successful career in broadcast radio and is a motivational speaker today. He now holds the professional speaking designation of CSP, which is held by less than 8 percent of the professional speakers in the world.

I told him he was amazing. He responded, "I don't think I'm amazing. I'm normal." Some might think that Alvin's perception of himself as normal is only a method of coping, but it's much more than that. It's the way he leads his life and the philosophy he practices every day. The power and sincerity of Alvin's beliefs was proven in 1991 when he met a beautiful young woman named Darlene. She had previously been married to a man she described as very handsome and extremely athletic. Yet, Alvin won her affection over her other suitors. When I asked Darlene how she felt at first about dating a man with no arms, she said, "He didn't win me over because of what he doesn't have. He won me because of what he does have that so many other men don't." I asked what that was and she replied, "Confidence and an extremely high self-worth." They've been married since 1993 and Alvin contributes much of his business success today to meeting Darlene and their learning to work together so well. He humbly refers to himself as the talent and Darlene as the brains of his business, but I know they're both very smart and talented. Alvin's meekness is yet another sign of what a strong individual he is.

The Little Cheerleader Who Took a Bullet and Kept on Kicking

While giving a seminar in Rome, Georgia, I met a lovely young woman named Tonya Hurston. She looked like a stereotypical Southern Belle who you might expect to see sitting on a veranda, sipping a Mint Julep, and living a life of luxury. You wouldn't think she had a care in the world. She seems like the kind of person who came from a good family, had an uneventful childhood, and has led a charmed life. While she'll tell you that she did come from a good family and has led a charmed life, her childhood was anything but uneventful.

Tonya was an extremely active child and the most enthusiastic cheerleader at her school. Her family moved to a different town three hours away as she was starting the sixth grade. Her brother took her out into the woods to teach her how to shoot a new gun three days after moving. After retrieving cans to serve as targets, she felt her arm suddenly go limp and numb. She looked down and saw blood "shooting like a fountain" out of her chest. The unthinkable had happened. Her brother's gun had accidentally gone off and she had been shot. He immediately applied direct pressure to stop the bleeding and rushed her back to the house. Her parents took her to three different hospitals that night. Her right arm had turned black by the time she got to the third. She was rushed into emergency surgery. She received a blood transfusion and was told that the nerves to her arm were completely severed. Later, the surgeons wanted to amputate. She refused to consent even though they swore she would never move her arm from the shoulder down. What she remembers most now at age 28 is asking her mother that night, "Am I going to die?" She made it through the first surgery with the bullet still in place. It eventually worked its way to the skin's surface and was removed about a year later. By then she could move her shoulder but was still unable to move her arm.

The community banded together and raised money to send Tonya and her parents to a Boston surgeon who could possibly reattach the nerves. They made the trip with high hopes that were soon dashed when he told them she had less than a 50 percent chance of surviving the surgery. He refused to perform such a risky procedure. They returned to Georgia devastated and anticipating a life for Tonya without the use of her right arm. What the doctors didn't know was how determined this little girl was. She continued physical therapy with an intensity unknown to most adults. Her first goal was to simply raise her wrist. She reached this first milestone one proud day when she could raise her wrist and hold it for three seconds. There wasn't a dry eye in the room. Those short three seconds of Tonya's life were a preamble of what was to come. She had missed cheerleading her seventh grade year and swore to return to cheerleading before her eighth grade year was over. This presented a major challenge since she only had three months left in her eighth grade year. They told her it couldn't be done, but they didn't know Tonya's drive to succeed. She proved everyone wrong and proudly joined her cheerleading squad for the Central Middle School Lions' opening game of the 1989 football season. Today, Tonya and her husband Shawn own a thriving flooring business. I consulted with Tonya on a small business crisis and asked how she remained so even-keeled about it. She responded, "I believe God has a special purpose for me or I would not have survived the tragedy of a gunshot wound. God constantly reminds me that my problems aren't as bad as I think. There's always someone worse off. I have been truly blessed."

If you feel powerless over your career after reading these stories, I suggest that you quit reading this book until you make a life-changing decision. Decide if you're going to be a victim the rest of your life. There's no chance whatsoever you'll ever be a highly valued employee if you are. You'll be the first to be laid off when times get tough and the last one to ever get a raise. Note that Robyn, Alvin, and Tonya were more than highly valued employees. They each ended up owning their own businesses because they were so driven to succeed. They told me they made four conscious choices that changed their careers and their lives:

1. They would not be characterized by what happened to them.
2. They would not feel sorry for themselves.
3. They would never use the word "victim."
4. They would succeed in their careers and their lives.

You can't be anything you want to be. We all have limitations. I wanted to fly F-16s for the Air Force but couldn't because I don't have perfect vision and I'm too tall to eject from the cockpit. You can choose to succeed at what you're capable of doing. No matter what life has dealt you, you always have the choice of how you deal with it.

> Life is 10 percent what happens to me and 90 percent how I react to it.
>
> John C. Maxwell

Lose Your Fear of Failure

Perhaps the most crippling thing any of us can encounter is fear. Fear of failure truly paralyzes many. Highly valued employees understand the difference between failing and making mistakes. A mistake means something was done incorrectly or a wrong decision was made. It involves fault on someone's part. Failure doesn't mean anything was done wrong. Failure can occur when everything was done exactly as it should have been. Just as with mistakes, failure is inevitable. The more we strive to succeed, the more we fail. The definitions of success and failure may be opposite but they must coexist just as Democrats and Republicans. We cannot control failure, but we can control how we view it.

> Most great people have attained their greatest success just one step beyond their greatest failure.
>
> Napoleon Hill

Many great achievers failed before they reached success. Some even failed after succeeding. In addition to Walt Disney and Henry Ford, others who filed for bankruptcy include:

- Donald Trump (through Trump Hotels & Casino Resorts Inc.)
- Francis Ford Coppola, Oscar-winning director
- Henry Heinz, best known for Heinz 57 Varieties
- Mark Twain (Samuel Clemens)
- Oscar Wilde, poet and author
- P. T. Barnum
- Rembrandt, the famous Dutch painter
- Ulysses S. Grant, eighteenth president and the face on the $50 bill
- William Fox, cofounder of Twentieth Century Fox Studios

Milton Hershey founded two candy companies that failed before founding what is now Hershey's Food Corporation, maker of Hershey's Chocolate. Still other great achievers were discouraged from pursuing their dreams but did so anyway. Some of the most successful people and ideas were discouraged by people who predicted failure. Examples include:

> The concept is interesting and well-formed, but to earn better than a C, the idea must be feasible.
>
> A Yale professor in response to student
> Fred Smith's paper proposing reliable
> overnight delivery service.
> Mr. Smith later founded FedEx.

You'd better learn secretarial skills or else get married.

> Modeling agency, rejecting
> Marilyn Monroe in 1944

That rainbow song's no good. Take it out.

> An MGM memo after the first showing
> of *The Wizard of Oz*

Forget it. No Civil War picture ever made a nickel.

> An MGM executive advising against investing
> in *Gone with the Wind*

Can't act. Can't sing. Slightly bald. Can dance a little.

> A film company's comments on Fred Astaire's
> 1928 screen test

This telephone has too many shortcomings to be seriously considered as a means of communication. The device is inherently of no value to us.

> An internal Western Union memo in 1876

You must be willing to risk failure in order to succeed. This means taking chances and not always playing it safe.

In order to succeed, your desire for success should be greater than your fear of failure.

> Bill Cosby

Avoid Little Man Syndrome

One form of learned helplessness many Americans have developed is "little man syndrome." This has nothing to do with physical stature. They see themselves as very small fish that don't stand a chance of thriving in a big sea. Comments such as "The little man just can't get ahead" become a self-fulfilling prophesy. Most people are small in the business world when compared to Donald Trump or Bill Gates, yet even starting small is no excuse for little man syndrome. John Schnatter was a little guy in his industry when he began making pizza in the broom closet of his father's tavern in 1984. Domino's already had over 1,000 stores and Pizza Hut had over 4,000. Had John told anyone that he was going to take on Pizza Hut and Domino's, they might have told him that the little man can't get ahead. He took on Pizza Hut and Domino's and experienced the true potential of thinking big in 1997 when Pizza Hut cofounder Frank Carney began buying Papa John's franchises.

Too many people see their companies as all-powerful and see themselves as powerless. They think they're at the whim of the company. They don't realize it's actually the other way around. Companies have no power without good employees.

> In the end, all business operations can be reduced to three words; people, product, and profits. Unless you've got a good team, you can't do much with the other two.
>
> Lee Iacocca

Some people are so entrenched in this thinking that they develop a "we versus them" mentality. I've met people who actually believe managers enjoy firing people. I will set the record straight right here and now in case one of those people happens to read this book. Managers get no pleasure from firing people. They're often overwhelmed with feelings of guilt, failure, and sadness. Managers fail when employees fail. Your boss wants you to succeed.

An engineer from San Francisco who sat beside me on a flight to Dallas argued that her boss couldn't care less about whether she succeeds. She claimed that he was a lazy jerk who didn't care about anyone but himself and wanted her to fail. She missed the big picture. He doesn't want her to fail even if he is as she described him.

Her failure would mean more work for him. He needs her to succeed at her job so that he won't have to do the job himself.

What If Your Company Doesn't Recognize Your Value?

People sometimes ask what they should do if their company doesn't
pay them what they're worth. Go out and interview if you believe the
market is paying more than you're making. Good managers know
that workers won't be highly motivated if they're underpaid. No employer wants to lose a highly valued employee and most will match
other offers if you're truly worth more than you're being paid. Always
knowing what you're worth in the free market is another example of
taking charge of your own destiny. Don't expect your employer to do
this for you. You may also discover that you're making more at your
present job than others are paying. This is still helpful because you
need to know what you have in order to appreciate it.

Some argue that their employers are greedy, dishonest, or
crooked. My response to this is, "If you're willing to work for an organization like that, what does this say about you?" They then often
claim there are no other jobs out there and that they're forced to
work for the allegedly greedy, dishonest, or crooked employer. This
is the vicious cycle of learned helplessness. If you truly believe there
are no other jobs out there, you better:

- Be grateful you have the only job there is.
- Make sure you keep your job since it's the only one there is.
- Become a highly valued employee.

Opportunity Only Knocks Once

Sometimes people are so busy whining about how little opportunity
there is that they don't hear opportunity when it knocks. Microsoft
exists today only because Bill Gates and Paul Allen heard a very faint
tapping that many would have missed. That faint tap was the most
profitable opportunity the world has ever known. Gates and Allen
learned to program big commercial computers as students at Lake-
side prep school in Seattle in the late 1960s. In 1974, Allen was on

his way to visit Gates who was then a student at Harvard University. He picked up a copy of *Popular Electronics* magazine that would change the world. The headline read "World's First Microcomputer Kit to Rival Commercial Models." A New Mexico company named Micro Instrumentation and Telemetry Systems (MITS) had introduced the world's first mini-computer called the Altair. It was so crude that it had no monitor, keyboard, or software. Gates called MITS and told them he and Allen had a software program that could run on the Altair. They were invited to come demonstrate it. The problem was that they hadn't yet written such a program and didn't even have an Altair. They had never even seen one except in the magazine. They were simply convinced that they had an opportunity they couldn't let slip away. They worked around the clock to write the program and had it ready to go eight weeks later. Allen flew to Albuquerque to demonstrate it but didn't know if it would work. He programmed his first Altair in the office at MITS and it worked perfectly. Gates dropped out of Harvard to form Microsoft with Allen in 1975 when he was barely more than a teenager.

Opportunity knocked again nearly 20 years later and Bill Gates almost missed it this time. In the early 1990s, he thought the Internet was just a passing fad and decided not to pursue it. He later realized he was wrong but not until it was very late in the game. Netscape Navigator already had 90 percent of the market share in Internet browsers by the time Microsoft released the first version of Internet Explorer in 1995. Internet Explorer wasn't widely used until Version 4 was integrated with Windows 98. Today, Microsoft owns about 85 percent of the market share for Internet browsers.

> Opportunity is missed by most people because it is dressed in overalls and looks like work.
>
> Thomas Edison

You must grab opportunity the moment it presents itself regardless of whether you're starting small or are already the wealthiest man in the world. The greatest irony about opportunity is that it often presents itself at the least opportune time. Bill Gates' parents didn't want him to drop out of Harvard to pursue his passion for computers. It would have been far more convenient if the opportunity to launch Microsoft presented itself after he graduated.

I experienced a similar scenario as an author. There are millions of books in print today and authors are a dime a dozen. Personal computers have made self-publishing so easy that it now seems like everyone has written a book. The big challenge is to get published and to do so with a major publisher. After self-publishing for about 10 years, I received an e-mail in August 2004 that changed my life. It was from an editor at John Wiley & Sons and they wanted to publish me. Past authors Wiley has published include Elizabeth Barrett Browning, Washington Irving, Edgar Allen Poe, Charles Dickens, and Herman Melville. This was a very big deal for me. I signed a contract two months later to write my first book for Wiley.

Writing a book is a daunting proposition. It's extremely tedious, time-consuming, and lonely. The workload is unbelievable. There's research and citations in addition to the actual writing. Every study mentioned must include details such as the date the study was conducted and the names of the researchers involved. Every time the title of another book is mentioned, the publisher, date, author, and city must be cited. Then comes the editing and rewrites. Editors have to correct the grammatical mistakes, suggest content to add or delete, correct factual errors, and make the material politically correct enough to be commercially viable. They have to catch the tiniest details the average person would never think about. For example, I used the term "workman's compensation" in my first manuscript. I had no idea this is now referred to as "worker's compensation." Terms must be gender neutral. This is why "stewardess" or "steward" is now "flight attendant" and "waiter" or "waitress" is now "server." I also told a story about self-discipline and going to dinner at Outback Steakhouse in my first manuscript. I wrote that the waitress brought out the Bloomin' Onion, placed it right under your nose, and your dinner companion ordered Outback's Cinnamon Apple Oblivion for dessert. Three edits were made to that one statement by the time the book made it to print. The first edit was to change waitress to "server." The second was that the proper placement of a Bloomin' Onion is in the center of the table, not under anyone's nose. The third was the Cinnamon Apple Oblivion. I had recently tried this dessert and thought it was appropriate for the story. I later discovered that Outback had discontinued this item, so it was replaced with their Chocolate Thunder from Down Under. Imagine doing this for a 60,000-word manuscript and you'll get an idea of what's involved in writing a book that gets published.

The contract for the first book was signed on October 20, 2004. That was my birthday and the contract was a great birthday present. It called for me to submit the manuscript by February 10, 2005. The time frame would have been no big deal if I were at home or in my office. But I'm on a speaking circuit that takes me on the road every other week. This effectively cut the four months to write the book down to two. Then my editor sent me an e-mail on the second week of November asking if I'd like to write a book on performance evaluations. I jumped at the opportunity to write another book. He asked what time frame I'd like for that one and offered as much as a year. Without thinking, I chose the same date as the first book. This cut the time available to write the first book in half again. The following months were not pleasant ones. The hours were very long, sleep was rare, and the work was intense. It was similar to the time when Bill Gates and Paul Allen wrote the software that launched Microsoft.

The final twist of irony is that today the second book outsells the first book. I am so glad that I seized the opportunity when it presented itself and didn't wait until a time when it was more convenient.

Conclusion

Choose to spend your life as a victim, feeling sorry for yourself, or believing you're powerless leads to helplessness. You can't be a highly valued employee if you're helpless. Seize opportunities whenever they present themselves and never complain that there are no opportunities out there. Just look more closely. You have the power to control your destiny.

CHAPTER 17

Become a Problem Solver

Number one quality of a good employee: They need to be problem solvers, not problem creators.

Mike Anderson, Owner, Cedar Rapids
Animal Hospital , Cedar Rapids, Iowa

There are two types of people we can surround ourselves with when we face problems. One is the type who remains silent while we cry on his or her shoulder. This feels good at the time but accomplishes nothing other than allowing us to continue in our pity party. It also requires no effort or caring from the other person. Bartenders, enablers, codependent people, and even dogs fall into this category. When we experience problems, we should turn to people who will have empathy but also hold us accountable for solving our own problems. These include family members who truly love us and real friends who truly care about us. When someone truly cares about us, he or she doesn't want to see us suffer.

There are five types of people when it comes to creating problems:

1. Those who create problems and ignore them. Addicts fall into this category.

2. Those who create problems and expect someone else to solve them. They know the problem must be dealt with but they won't make the effort to do it.
3. Those who solve their own problems.
4. Those who solve their own problems and also help others solve theirs.
5. Those who solve their own problems, help others solve theirs, and also prevent problems.

Business is about solving problems. The better your problem-solving skills are, the more valuable you will be to your employer. It's important to note that the highly valued employee often creates more problems than the lowly valued employee does. This is because the highly valued employee takes more initiative, accomplishes more, and also fails more. The number of problems you create or mistakes you make isn't what counts most; it's the number of solutions you find.

> A good employee is someone who seeks out ways to streamline business functions, whether it's easier ways to handle paper traffic, phone calls, or procedures.
>
> Melissa Hutcheson, Statewide Realty,
> Montgomery, Alabama

Problem-Solving Skills Can Be More Useful than Technical Knowledge

I spent quite a bit of time on the phone with technical support when I first began using personal computers in the late 1980s. I recently considered calling a company's technical support department for help while struggling with a computer problem. I realized I hadn't done this for over a decade and asked myself why this was. It's certainly not that my technical knowledge has grown so exponentially. I have above average computer skills but have not kept up as technology has grown by leaps and bounds. I considered that it might be because men don't read directions. As politically incorrect as this stereotype may be, I fit it perfectly. Being able to call an expert and have him or her spoon-feed me solutions is perfect for someone who doesn't like to read directions. I'd be more than willing to pay whatever price such a convenience costs. I don't call tech support because I have completely lost faith in the concept. I've come to expect them not to know the answer or to give me the wrong answer.

The problem I was trying to solve centered on a color printer. Each computer in my company has a black-and-white laser printer attached directly to it and a network links the computers. There's one color printer that is attached directly to my office manager's computer. I was unable to print from my wireless laptop computer to the color printer and decided to purchase an adaptor to connect the printer directly to the network hub. I went to a local computer store and explained what I needed to one of its associates. He took a product off the shelf and I bought it. When I retuned to my office, I discovered that he had sold me the wrong item. I was quite frustrated that my problem wasn't solved. Then I was frustrated that I had wasted so much time. Then I was angry at the clerk.

I asked myself what part I played in this situation. Was there something I was doing wrong or failing to do right? Was it foolish to trust an employee of one of the country's leading computer retailers to understand what I was asking for? I decided it wasn't. It's reasonable for any customer to expect businesses to train their employees how to answer customers' questions correctly and admit when they don't know the answers so that customers can ask someone who might know.

The person who eventually solved the problem wasn't a computer specialist; it was my office manager. I expressed my frustration to her about having bought the wrong device and then went back to my desk to try to solve the problem. She walked into my office about 10 minutes later and said, "Try to print to the color laser from your laptop now." I did and it worked. She had discovered that the only problem was that the printer wasn't set to be shared in Microsoft Windows XP. I looked for an easy mechanical fix I could buy in a box while she examined the problem and found the best solution. While she's more technically literate than most administrative employees, it wasn't technical literacy that fixed the problem. The employee at the computer store probably had a high level of technical literacy. What allowed my office manager to fix the problem was that she:

- Cared more than the store clerk did
- Had more patience than me
- Had highly developed problem-solving skills that allowed her to methodically think through the situation

I made three mistakes in my attempt to fix the problem:

1. I was impatient and looking for a quick fix.
2. I was trying to buy a solution instead of figuring it out.
3. I looked to a source with the best technical skills when I should have looked to a source with the best problem-solving skills.

> Our best employees are those who try to think of solutions when they are presented with problems.
>
> Sandra Vaughn, Child and Adolescent
> Service Center, Canton, Ohio

Preventing Problems Makes You an Even More Highly Valued Employee

Recently, I asked my office manager to find a source for plastic CD holders for a new self-study kit I will be offering. I returned from a seminar in Indianapolis and a sample from a plastic manufacturer in Minneapolis was on my desk. It was perfect except for one tiny detail. The plastic sleeve stuck out from the binder by two inches. I put it back on her desk with a note that read:

> Won't work for obvious reasons. Proceed to Plan B.
> P.S. I don't know what Plan B is, so let me know when you figure it out.

A sample from a manufacturer in Chicago was on my desk within 72 hours. It fit perfectly and had a note attached that read:

Plan B didn't work either, so I didn't bother sharing it with you. This is Plan C and I've already filled out the purchase order for 1,000 of these puppies. Let me know when it's okay to release it.

Intellectuals solve problems, geniuses prevent them.

Albert Einstein

Is It Possible for Everyone to Become a Problem Solver?

Some people insist that it's not possible for them to make a difference in their company. I would question why the company is paying them if that were truly the case. Their departure would probably go unnoticed if they can't make a difference. You don't have to solve huge problems to make a difference. Every tiny problem you solve still makes you that much more valuable to your employer. The following are examples of highly valued employees who set out to make a difference and did.

Belmont University Employees Cut Through the Red Tape

Students at Belmont University in Nashville were accustomed to long lines at the business office. They had to go to one office to fill out enrollment forms, another office on a different part of campus to fill out more forms, and were sometimes told they needed to go back where they started. A group of highly valued Belmont employees set out to solve the problem. The solution was as efficient as it was simple. They began training coordinators to deal with all administrative aspects and then located them in one building called Belmont Central. The system was so successful that other colleges have now emulated it.

Employees of a New York Hospital Solve the Need for Speed

Albany Medical Center in New York was well known for its expertise and success with kidney transplants. It was also known for its kidney transplant patients spending over two weeks in the hospital in recovery. This was about a week longer than the national average. A group of highly valued employees in the renal transplant unit decided to solve the problem. They reviewed each step of every procedure and created a "pathway" to get patients home sooner. Their pathway cut average hospital stay for a kidney transplant patient to eight days, increased the rate of patients who survived one year after surgery from 87 percent to 97 percent, reduced costs per patient by 25 percent, and reduced re-admission rates by 50 percent.

How Highly Valued Navy Employees
Kept Fighter Jets Flying

The North Island Naval Air Depot in San Diego makes replacement parts, repairs, and overhauls aviation systems of Navy and Marine Corp aircraft. Their mission is to help these war birds "Reign supreme and return in glory." Years ago, part of the facility was anything but glorious. Building 472 was known as the black hole where airplane parts and money disappeared forever. Captain Charles Sapp created a team of 10 employees drawn from each department and presented them with a daunting challenge. They had to turn around the money-losing operation or else it would be closed and hundreds of employees would lose their jobs. Highly valued employee and team leader Deborah Vergos began the process by meeting with team members for two days on a local college campus so they could brainstorm. She began by asking the team to make a list of reasons their costs were so high, work quality was so low, and turnaround time was so bad. They came up with a list of 70 reasons and pared it down to the core. One problem was that morale was so low that ugly rivalries occurred. Finger pointing led to departments spending more time blaming each other than solving problems. Another problem was that management wasn't listening to employees. There was also no control system in place. Customers would order parts they never received and often not get billed when they did receive them. Some customers literally walked into the building, took the parts they needed, and walked away. They were losing $3 million a year because customers weren't paying for parts and work.

Vergos began by giving workers something they hadn't experienced before—a chance to speak up. She asked them what they needed to do their jobs more effectively and she listened. Some workers needed new tools so she bought them. She rearranged desks in one room to force team members to communicate. They started meeting with customers every week and asking how they could serve them better. It hadn't been uncommon in the past for a $20 million F/A-18 Hornet fighter jet to sit idly in a hangar for weeks while waiting for a part that cost less than $1. Vergos's team set up a Quick-Access Center to ensure basic parts were delivered within 10 days. The operation became so successful that they began competing against private firms to make F/A-18 parts and won contracts.

Highly Valued Basket Weavers in Ohio

The Longaberger Company of Newark, Ohio, is known worldwide for its high-quality handmade baskets. It has 67,000 sales consultants located throughout all 50 states. The weavers in Longaberger's plant are paid based on production. Over 2,000 of these talented artisans produce tens of thousands of baskets per day. It costs employees and the company money when weavers have to stop to look for supplies. Three highly valued employees set out to fix this problem. Merrill Stout, Greg Whiteman, and Brian Tigner discovered that weavers were sometimes not getting the correct material to make the basket style they had been assigned. Employees were sometimes forced to borrow material from coworkers. This contributed to variances in productivity by as much as 400 percent. The team took a paid leave from the plant floor to study flowcharting, cause-and-effect analysis, and other industrial engineering issues. They also trained to use each piece of equipment to better understand what other workers experienced. They then studied 40 other basket weavers for 19 days to determine what the biggest problem was. They found that some of the recycled material was too dry or moldy to use and invented a system that reduced the amount of incorrect or unacceptable material the weavers received. The results were dramatic. Each weaver put out a flag to indicate when material was needed. Over 52 flags were put out on an average day before the new system was implemented. That figure dropped to about 9 after the new system was implemented. This resulted in a savings of about $3 million.

NSA Employees Eliminate a Bureaucratic Nightmare

The National Security Agency (NSA) in Washington, DC, is so secretive that it's sometimes called "No Such Agency." Its job is to protect our country from spies. Yet, despite its high-tech equipment and highly trained intelligence and counterintelligence personnel, it fell victim to an enemy that incapacitates many government agencies—red tape. A group of six highly valued employees undertook the task of fixing a problem that was 30 years in the making. The problem was an antiquated travel system that took up to a month and a half to reimburse employees for travel expenses. To make the situation worse, NSA employees spent over eight hours on average complying with NSA regulations each time they traveled. They estimated this cost the agency over

$8 million a year. This meant over eight million taxpayer dollars were being wasted. The employees studied private sector companies such as IBM and Apple. They found that these companies processed many more claims in a tiny fraction of the time. The NSA employees created a system using an outside travel agency to handle travel arrangements for NSA employees. Only one manager now has to approve travel instead of five in the previous system. The expense voucher employees now fill out is one page instead of six in the previous system. The total time for reimbursement of employee travel expenses dropped from a month and a half to less than two days.

Ohio State University Employees Turn around a Bus System

Ohio State University in Columbus sprawls over 1,700 acres, has over 50,000 students, and over 20,000 employees. Traffic jams became a common event and parking spaces were so hard to come by that people actually got into fistfights. A team of 16 employees was given the responsibility to solve the problem and only three months to do it. The team began by interviewing students and faculty and then hired a consultant. They completely redesigned the bus routes so that they ran in both directions. This cut the maximum bus ride from 30 minutes to 7. The next challenge was convincing more people to utilize the buses. They solved this problem by getting professors, coaches, and the university president to ride the bus. They increased utilization even more by getting the biggest VIP on campus to also ride. OSU alumnus and athletic director Archie Griffin is the only two-time winner of the prestigious Heisman Trophy award. When students and faculty saw him on the bus, it made riding the bus as chic as chic could be.

Postal Employees Save the USPS a Bundle

Employees of the Royal Oak, Michigan, mail distribution center sorted over four million pieces of mail every day from 160 area post offices. Bags and trays of mail are dropped off in the afternoon and then sorted by zip code. The mail is supposed to leave shortly after midnight. The problem was that odd shaped mail slowed the process down so much that next day deliveries weren't making it by the next day. A group of highly valued employees took on the task of solving this problem. They found that nearly one-third of the mail that was being manually sorted could have been sorted by machine. Employees who manually sorted mail were sending pieces they thought should be automated back up the line and it was coming back to them. The repetitive loop caused double handling of mail and was delaying delivery by as much as a week. The team first set up better training procedures for clerks to check mail that was rejected by the machine and refeeding it to the sorter when possible. They also created better training procedures for manual sorters to help know when to send mail back. They anticipated saving $380,000 the first year. They saved over $700,000.

The Doorman Who Went the Extra Mile—For 16 Hours

Keith DeBiase is a doorman and valet captain at Nemacolin Woodlands Resort and Spa in Farmington, Pennsylvania. He has an uncanny ability to remember guests by their names even when he hasn't seen them in years. He also remembers the preferences of each guest. He often quotes Eleanor Roosevelt, "People will forget what you say, people will forget what you do, people will never forget how you make them feel." He also understands that the resort has a problem when guests have a problem. When a family of seven was staying at his resort and their car had to be towed, Keith solved their problem of getting home. He drove them home, all the way to New York. What's most revealing about what a highly valued employee Keith is lies in what he did when he returned from the trip. He didn't take the next day off even though it would have been understandable. He returned to work on time the next day and helped the resort with another problem they faced—setting up for a big event.

The Game Warden Who Brought in Millions

After over a quarter century as a Texas game warden, James Connally of Brownwood found himself facing the most formidable animal alive—humans who owe money. Warden Connally was made interim manager of the Civil Restitution Program and posted numbers the Internal Revenue Service would be proud of. He increased the voluntary collection rate from 31 percent to 68 percent despite the fact that some of the debts were over a decade old. He oversaw nearly $2 million in revenue collected for his agency. He wasn't so successful because he had a background in collecting accounts receivable. His background was in dealing with wildlife and collecting debt was the last thing he wanted to do. He was successful because he gives 100 percent at whatever he does even if it's not exactly what he prefers to do.

The Honeywell Engineers Whose Idea Was Worth Millions

Engineers are often faced with technical problems so they're well equipped to find solutions. A problem that engineers at Honeywell in Torrance, California, faced seemed insurmountable. An ozone converter used on the Boeing 777 that was supposed to last three years was wearing out in just 12 months. This converter takes outside air at high altitudes and makes it breathable for passengers inside the cabin. A team of highly valued employees was assembled from the aerospace environmental controls division in Torrance, Boeing's commercial division in Everett, Washington, and Honeywell's technical center in Des Plaines, Illinois. They first looked for a temporary solution to buy time while they found a permanent one. This entailed figuring out a way to clean the used converters and get them back in service faster. They tried 32 different solutions and finally found a method that decreased turnaround time from one month to one week. This allowed the team more time to pursue a permanent solution. Jonathon Nunag, a highly valued employee for United Airlines, made arrangements to have a Boeing 777 fly back and forth over Oakland for six hours to evaluate the converter. Highly valued Honeywell employees Todd Funston and Andy Hamelynck worked 18-hour days testing the converters. As often happens when trying to solve problems, they discovered the solution was to look in another direction. The problem wasn't in the air; it was on the ground. Converters were wearing out prematurely because of dirty air on the ground caused in part from exhaust from other planes. The converter's capacity was increased to accommodate ground contamination and the problem was solved. This also allowed Honeywell to expand its market to other aircraft. Not only did these highly valued employees save a $20 million division; they also opened the door to another $10 million in new business.

The Waiter Who Makes Hawaiian Vacations Complete

Jose Racasa is a highly valued employee of the Radisson Hotel Waikiki Prince Kuhio in Honolulu. When guests mention the parts of Hawaii they missed out on during their vacation in paradise, Jose solves their problem by taking them on a personal mini-tour after work. It comes as no surprise to anyone that guests often return to the hotel because of Jose.

The W. Edwards Deming of Education

When Wilkerson Middle School in Birmingham, Alabama, moved sixth through eighth graders out of elementary school and into middle school, the results were disastrous. The idea was to prepare the pre-teens for high school but near anarchy occurred with students, teachers, and parents. Then highly valued employee Diane Rivers applied the principles of total quality management (TQM) guru W. Edwards Deming. She, along with the principal and two assistant principals found that poor reading skills was the worst problem and took an unusual approach to solve this problem. They created a program called Readers Anonymous in which six graders who didn't read well were tutored by seventh and eight graders who did. The results were phenomenal and not just for sixth graders. Reading scores jumped 21 percent for sixth graders in just one year. They also jumped 31 percent for seventh graders and 26 percent for eight graders. The TQM system also had a huge impact on other areas. Math scores rose 41 percent for sixth graders, 15 percent for seventh graders, and 4 percent for eighth graders, while suspensions fell by 84 percent.

Tennessee Valley Authority Employees Cut Out the Slag

The Tennessee Valley Authority (TVA) plant in Memphis burned high-sulphur coal with no problems for over 35 years. Then new Environmental Protection Agency regulations forced them to convert to low-sulphur coal and technical problems arose immediately. Slag buildup kept the coal from burning properly by clogging holes in the burners. It once shut the plant down for 10 days and resulted in a cost of $3 million in lost revenue and $500,000 in repairs. A group of highly valued employees took initiative to solve the problem. They found that the low-sulphur coal was coming from different sources and didn't burn in a consistent manner or at a consistent rate. They set up a system to test the coal before it left the mines, in train rail cars, and while still on barges. They then used computers to track the incoming coal and adjust the burners when the coal arrived. Shutdown losses dropped 80 percent the first year this system was in place and they saved $3 million by combining coal from two states. They also dropped the emissions levels so far that the county could allow new industries to move to town again and generate badly needed tax revenues.

We are continually faced by great opportunities brilliantly disguised as insoluble problems.

Lee Iacocca

Conclusion

Business is all about solving problems. Every new problem that presents itself creates an opportunity for you to become a highly valued employee. Notice in the stories of the highly valued employees in this chapter that their jobs were completely unrelated. There were surgeons, basket weavers, engineers, clerks, housekeepers, law enforcement officers, and postal employees. Yet, they had three common traits. First, they all had the desire to solve problems their organizations faced. Second, they succeeded in solving those problems. Third, each earned a reputation for being a highly valued employee because of his or her problem-solving skills.

CHAPTER 18

Avoid the Four Career Killers

Never mistake motion for action.

Ernest Hemingway

In Chapters 1 through 17 we looked at the steps you should take to become a highly valued employee. Even when you take each of these steps and make all the right moves, just one wrong move can undermine everything. Some argue that negating many years of faithful service because of one small misstep is unfair. They're wrong. Different institutions treat "small missteps" in extremely different ways. A law-abiding citizen who's never had so much as a speeding ticket in 40 years of driving can be convicted of manslaughter and put in prison for running just one stop sign and causing the accidental death of another driver. At the same time, nearly every organized religion teaches that God can forgive that driver for the life he took.

Employment is more like the legal system. Just one mistake can sabotage your entire career regardless of how good your track record has been in the past. In this last chapter, we'll look at some of the specific mistakes a highly valued employee should never make.

My list of good qualities and skills starts with self-discipline and maturity. An employee is assigned a task and he completes it without constantly being reminded that it's his job and that he is responsible. I have a gentleman, Chris Fabrizio, who works for me. He completes his daily chores, performs his paramedic duties with efficiency and pride, and goes above his call of duty in many ways. He is the first to volunteer for an extra task. I know that when he is at work I don't have to baby sit. Things will be completed beyond satisfactory. He takes pride in his work and respects that he is being paid for doing a job. He respects authority and is not argumentative. He makes the most of his day and along with being a true gentleman and top-notch employee, he adds humor to the workplace. I wish I had 10 employees like him.

Carla Morris, Wetzel County Ambulance
Authority, New Martinsville, West Virginia

Career Killer One: Confusing Activity with Productivity

People often make the mistake of going through the motions without focusing on what they should be accomplishing even when they're not consciously faking it. We've all heard the "work smarter not harder" cliché. The problem with working smarter is that it requires more mental effort and some people are just mentally lazy. This is a hurdle advertisers must overcome with consumers. One advertising expert said, "Customers don't want you to give them a fish and they don't want you to teach them how to fish. They want you to catch the fish, cook it for them, cut it up for them, and then pre-chew it for them." Thinking requires effort. This is why it's often easier to give our brains a rest by turning them completely off while performing a task. Think about how many times you've driven past the exit for your own house because your mind was wandering somewhere else or was completely turned off.

Another place where people often confuse activity with progress is weight loss. Former yo-yo dieter Michelle May of Phoenix, Arizona, told me that millions of people will measure their food; buy foods they wouldn't ordinarily eat; count calories, carbohydrates, or fat; and turn down invitations to dinner parties while dieting. All of this activity usually leads to temporary weight loss but results in no permanent progress because they haven't made the sustainable change in their thinking. She says that most people don't achieve the results they desire because they focus on the short-term activity instead of the long-term results. Michelle knows this because she's not only a former yo-yo dieter; she is also a respected medical doctor and author of the highly acclaimed book *Am I Hungry?*[1] Dr. May helps people lose weight without dieting by focusing on the process instead of just the activity.

I worked nights in the electronics department of a major retail store when I was in high school. One night I finished my tasks early and had nothing to do for the remaining hour of my shift. I was standing on the sales floor watching television when my general manager walked by and asked why I wasn't doing anything. I explained and he told me to just look busy. This approach might have been okay for a teenage part-time employee in the 1970s but it's not okay for an adult in the twenty-first century. You must actually be accomplishing a task while at work or you're not actually working. Highly valued employees must understand the difference between being on the clock and actually accomplishing something. Focus on results, not activity.

> Being busy doesn't always mean real work. The object of all work is production or accomplishment. Seeming to do is not doing.
>
> Thomas Edison

Career Killer Two: Giving Ultimatums

We've all heard the metaphor of children who threaten to take their marbles and go home if they can't get their way. Lowly valued employees behave the same way. They'll often threaten to quit if they don't get something they want, such as a raise. Highly valued employees understand that giving ultimatums always backfires. The employee who gets what he wants using ultimatums will create hostility even if management gives in to the request. I constantly teach managers to terminate employees who threaten to quit if they don't get what they want, no matter how reasonable the request may be. Managers refer to employees who give ultimatums as terrorists. Terrorists are people who get what they want by threatening to cause harm. Civilized societies know better than to negotiate with terrorists because it doesn't work. To negotiate, all parties must be trustworthy enough to keep their word to do what they promise to do. Terrorists don't keep their word because they lack integrity. Highly valued employees have integrity and know better than to create feelings of hostility with anyone.

Career Killer Three: Breaking the Chain of Command

People often ask me how they should proceed when their boss is a real jerk. My answer is to always be professional even when the boss isn't. You must be a good soldier and follow orders even when you don't agree with them. As discussed in Chapter 12, then Secretary of State Colin Powell disagreed with President Bush about how to proceed in Iraq. Yet, he followed orders as a good soldier does. Lowly valued employees make the mistake of going over their boss's head whenever they don't like something the boss has said or done. Highly valued employees understand that the chain of command should not be broken casually.

Career Killer Four: Failing to Have a Sense of Duty

My ninth-grade English teacher once asked for volunteers to help with the Junior/Senior prom. I raised my hand and asked, "What's in it for me?" I was never as humiliated as when I heard her answer. She looked straight at me and said in front of the entire class, "It's not about you Glenn. When you grow up, you'll learn that sometimes in life you have to do things for others out of a sense of duty. This is why young men volunteered to serve in Viet Nam and Korea." I still remember that look of disappointment and disgust in her eyes when I uttered those fateful words. Neither of us would have ever guessed that "It's not about you" would become the catch phrase for the best-selling book in the history of the world[2] other than the Bible. I was being a self-centered little brat and should have known

better. I was also a Boy Scout who later made it all the way to Eagle
Scout. Every Monday night our troop would begin our weekly meetings by reciting the Boy Scout pledge. The first lines are:

> On my honor, I will do my best,
> To do my duty to God and my country.

I don't know what I was thinking the day I blurted out that comment. To teach me a lesson, my teacher made me read General Douglas MacArthur's Thayer Award speech and write a report on it. It is
often referred to as the "Duty, Honor, Country speech" and is considered to be one of the most important speeches ever given by an
American, along with John F. Kennedy's "Ask not what your country
can do for you, ask what you can do for your country" and Lincoln's
Gettysburg address. It is, in my never-to-be-humble opinion, the
greatest speech ever given by anyone. I've never read words so compelling as those General MacArthur used in his address to the
cadets of West Point in accepting the award on May 12, 1962. The
following is an excerpt:

> Duty, honor, country: Those three hallowed words reverently dictate
> what you ought to be, what you can be, what you will be. They teach
> you to be proud and unbending in honest failure, but humble and gen-
> tle in success; not to substitute words for actions, not to seek the path
> of comfort, but to face the stress and spur of difficulty and challenge;
> to learn to stand up in the storm, but to have compassion on those who
> fall; to master yourself before you seek to master others; to have a heart
> that is clean, a goal that is high; to learn to laugh, yet never forget how
> to weep; to reach into the future, yet never neglect the past; to be seri-
> ous, yet never to take yourself too seriously; to be modest so that you
> will remember the simplicity of true greatness, the open mind of true
> wisdom, the meekness of true strength.
>
> The soldier, above all other men, is required to practice the great-
> est act of religious training—sacrifice. However hard the incidents of
> war may be, the soldier who is called upon to offer and to give his life
> for his country is the noblest development of mankind.
>
> Let civilian voices argue the merits or demerits of our processes of
> government: Whether our strength is being sapped by deficit financing
> indulged in too long, by Federal paternalism grown too mighty, by

power groups grown too arrogant, by politics grown too corrupt, by crime grown too rampant, by morals grown too low, by taxes grown too high, by extremists grown too violent; whether our personal liberties are as thorough and complete as they should be.

These great national problems are not for your professional participation or military solution. Your guidepost stands out like a ten-fold beacon in the night: Duty, honor, country.

I've kept a copy of the full speech for nearly 30 years and read it periodically. It sends shivers down my spine each time I do. The most intriguing part is that it's just as applicable today as it was over 40 years ago. The societal problems General MacArthur mentioned such as budget deficits, a federal government that might be too strong for its own good, special interest groups' influence on politicians, public corruption, crime, declining morality, taxes, violent extremists, and loss of personal liberties haven't changed. His advice to help West Point graduates succeed in 1962 also applies today and to civilians. Notice the principles he mentioned:

- Be humble in success.
- Be modest.
- Don't seek the path of least resistance.
- Duty.
- Be proud in honest failure.
- Learn how to face stress, difficulty, and challenge.
- Learn to sacrifice.
- Master yourself before trying to conquer others.
- Never substitute words for actions.
- Set your goals high.
- Stand strong.

The biggest career killer of all is failing to understand your duty to your employer. A duty means you're obligated to do something, and businesses are built on obligations to serve. Workers are obligated to serve their companies and companies are obligated to serve their customers. Forget this one principle and everything else will be irrelevant. Even the biggest and best run companies deal with this principle every day. UPS currently employs over 384,000 people, making it the third largest employer in the world. It is legendary for how well it takes care of its employees. UPS is also legendary for holding its employees to the highest standards and putting them through meticulous training. Their drivers are even taught which finger to hold a key ring on to save time. Their executives could easily afford to be a bit pompous. Instead, they teach and practice the values of humility, equality, and service to others, which were personal values of company founder Jim Casey. This can be seen in their recent change of slogans. This corporate giant changed from "We run the tightest ship in the shipping business" to "What can Brown do for you?" CEO Mike Eskew said, "This is where we have staked our future."

> What makes a good employee? It's never about them and what you can do for them. They are always asking what they can do for you. It's never I, it's WE.
>
> > Bonnie Kelly, Credit Manager, the *Star News*,
> > Wilmington, North Carolina

> One of the qualities of a good employee is not worrying about what's in it for them.
>
> > Betty Mallen, RN, Director of Planning
> > and Development, Hancock County Public
> > Health Services, Garner, Iowa

> If you take care of your company, your company will take care of you.
>
> > Robert R. Young Jr., Lanier Worldwide, Inc.,
> > Savannah, Georgia

Conclusion

Success is a habit, not an event. Since the average person will spend half a century working, success is the most profitable habit you can form. The sooner you develop this habit, the more profitable you will be. It all starts with making the decision. You are where you are in your life right now because of the decisions you've made in your past. If you have a habit of making good decisions, you're probably a success. If you have a habit of making bad decisions, it's never too late to change.

Career success is simple but it's not easy. Work is tough and it's not a place for sissies. You've already taken the first step toward becoming indispensable to your employer if you purchased this book for yourself. Regardless of whether you bought it or it was a gift, you have now taken the second step by reading it. Now take the third step by consciously deciding that you want to become indispensable to your employer. The path has been clearly laid out for you and all you have to do is follow it. If you have ever sworn that you could succeed in your career if you just knew what to do, you now have no more excuses. You are literally holding your future in your hands.

I thank you for reading this book. It has been my honor and privilege to serve you, and I look forward to hearing your personal success story. Send it to my office through my web site at www.Work-Is-Not-For-Sissies.com and it may appear in my next book. You could inspire someone else to succeed. I hope I have inspired you to do the same.

Notes

Preface

1. John C. Maxwell, *The 21 Irrefutable Laws of Leadership* (Nashville, TN: Nelson Business, 1988).
2. Glenn Shepard, *How to Manage Problem Employees* (Hoboken, NJ: John Wiley & Sons, 2005).
3. Jim Collins, *Good to Great* (New York: HarperCollins, 2001).

Chapter 1: First, Understand Why You Need to Be Indispensable

1. 1 Timothy 6:10.
2. Rick Warren, *The Purpose Driven Life* (Grand Rapids, MI: Zondervan, 2002).
3. Ayn Rand, *Atlas Shrugged* (New York: Penguin Group, 1957).

Chapter 2: Learn What Your Boss Wants from You

1. John T. Malloy, *Dress for Success* (New York: Warner Books, 1988).
2. Charles J. Sykes, *Dumbing Down Our Kids: Why American Children Feel Good About Themselves But Can't Read, Write, or Add* (New York: St. Martins, 1995).
3. Bill Cosby, *Fatherhood* (New York: Penguin Group, 1986).
4. A Texas jury convicted Wanda Holloway of hiring a hit man to kill Verna Heath and her daughter Amber in 1991.
5. A Massachusetts jury convicted Thomas Junta of involuntary manslaughter for beating Michael Costin, the father of another hockey player, to death at a 2000 youth hockey game.

Chapter 3: Be Low Maintenance

1. Proverbs 13:24 and 19:18.

Chapter 4: Answer the Questions Your Boss Didn't Ask

1. Jeffrey Fox, *How to Become CEO* (New York: Hyperion, 1998).

Chapter 6: Act Like You Own the Place

1. Thomas J. Stanley and William D. Danko, *The Millionaire Next Door* (New York: Pocket Books, 1996).

Chapter 7: Treat Your Job Like It's Your Lifelong Career, Even If It's Only a Stepping Stone

1. Norman Vincent Peale, *The Power of Positive Thinking* (New York: Ballantine Books, 1996).

Chapter 8: Become the Most Reliable Person in Your Company

1. 2002 CCH Unscheduled Absence Survey. CCH is a Riverwoods, IL, based provider of tax and business law information.

Chapter 9: Learn the Right Way to Make Mistakes

1. Marcus B. Nashelsky and Christopher H. Lawrence, "Accuracy of Cause of Death Determination without Forensic Autopsy Examination," *American Journal of Forensic Medicine and Pathology*, vol. 24, no. 4, pp. 313–319, December 2003.

Chapter 10: Broaden Your Circle of Influence

1. Mark Victor Hansen and Jack Canfield, *Chicken Soup for the Soul* (Deerfield Beach, FL: Health Communications, 1993).
2. Sandy Forster, *How to Be Wildly Wealthy Fast* (Mooloolaba, Queensland, Australia: Universal Prosperity Pty, 2004).
3. Peggy McColl, *The 8 Proven Secrets to Smart Success* (Ottawa, Ontario, Canada: Destinies Publishing, 2002).
4. Peggy McColl, *On Being the Creator of Your Own Destiny* (Ottawa, Ontario, Canada: Destinies Publishing, 2002).
5. Peggy McColl, *On Being a Dog with a Bone* (Ottawa, Ontario, Canada: Destinies Publishing, 2003).
6. John Gray, *Men Are from Mars, Women Are from Venus* (New York: HarperCollins, 1992).
7. John Gray, *What Your Mother Couldn't Tell You and Your Father Didn't Know* (New York: HarperCollins, 1994).

Chapter 11: Adopt the Work Ethic Your Grandparents Had

1. National Occupational Survey: Occupational Wages in the United States 2003, Summary 04-03.
2. Federal Housing Finance Board, monthly press release on November 30, 2004 (FHFB 04-43 MIRS).
3. For the sake of accuracy, I must note that I have been the driver of three new cars in my life. The first was a 1982 Camaro my father bought for me

while I was in college. The second was a 1989 Plymouth K-car my company bought new. Since I owned 50 percent of the stock in the corporation at that time, I technically owned half of a new car, although it was titled to the corporation. I also made the financial mistake of leasing a 1994 Eagle Vision for two years. I have driven three new cars but never bought one for myself.

4. Thomas J. Stanley and William D. Danko, *The Millionaire Next Door* (New York: Pocket Books, 1996).

Chapter 14: Take Charge of Your Own Destiny

1. Marcus Buckingham, *The One Thing You Need to Know* (New York: Free Press, 2002).
2. Marcus Buckingham, *First, Break All the Rules* (New York: Simon & Schuster, 1999).
3. Marcus Buckingham, *Now, Discover Your Strengths* (New York: Free Press, 2001).

Chapter 15: Don't Confuse Education with Knowledge

1. Dan Miller, *48 Days to the Work You Love* (Nashville, TN: Broadman & Holman, 2005).
2. Dave Ramsey, *Financial Peace* (New York: Viking Penguin, 2002).
3. Dave Ramsey, *The Total Money Makeover* (Nashville, TN: Thomas Nelson, 2003).

Chapter 16: Avoid Learned Helplessness

1. Victor Frankl, *Man's Search for Meaning* (New York: Pocket Books, 1997).
2. Dale Carnegie, *How to Win Friends and Influence People* (New York: Pocket Books, 1990).

Chapter 18: Avoid the Four Career Killers

1. Michelle May, *Am I Hungry?* (Phoenix, AZ: Nourish Publishing, 2004).
2. Rick Warren, *The Purpose Driven Life* (Grand Rapids, MI: Zondervan, 2002).

Index